Teaching STEM with Confidence:
Practical Tips and Strategies for New and Experienced Teachers

by Beverly Simmons

Edited by Alex Wayne Stripling, Jr.
Published by Printing Futures, Vancouver WA

ISBN 978-1-942357- 58-2
Hardcover Version

Photo permissions and authors, illustrators, designers, photographers available for download at the URL. http://www.PrintingFutures.com

Printing Futures
Publishing in Oregon

Teaching STEM with Confidence:
Practical Tips and Strategies for New and Experienced Teachers

Dedicated to Jeannie and Wayne who share my passions, pleasures, and problems with unconditional love and resilience, and to Hannah, who inspires me to share my stories!

Table of Contents

Forward: Meet a Passionate STEM Educator
This forward is written by Jeannie Ruiz, Executive Director, iNSL.

Beverly Simmons, a dedicated mother of three from a small town in southern GA, embarked on an inspiring journey to forge a fulfilling career in education and beyond. As a visionary and award-winning classroom teacher, she defied norms by creating an acclaimed program that integrated subjects in a multi-aged setting using data and analysis of project-based learning to teach a common core education, usually defined by non-integrated, stand-alone subjects. Beverly and her ground-breaking team employed innovative ideas such as using racing and remote-control cars to teach core subjects, while also innovating using computer-based mathematics to teach algebra years before they were common place in schools.

Development
Development: Early in her career, Beverly's innovative ideas were recognized by the Georgia Institute of Technology School of Computing and she was entrusted with leading the first year of the NSF funded Learning by Design curriculum project. Her success in this program led to her recruitment by Ford Motor Company, where she and her new company of engineers and educators established a Ford Technology Showcase Center next to the renowned Henry Ford Museum. Following this accomplishment, she and her engineering partner were selected by the Detroit Science Center Board to spearhead the design, build-out, and opening of the NEW Detroit Science Center Building, Exhibits, IMAX

Theater and Planetarium. It is on time and under budget opening captivated 32,000 visitors within its first 48-hour grand- opening. Beverly accepted the position of Vice President for the first year, staffed and managed sixty-five persons, and initiated the long-term program strategy for the venue.

Beverly's company of educators and engineers achieved significant milestones and awards. The team worked with owner, Gary Eaker, to design and build the AeroDYN Wind Tunnel in NC as they pioneered NASCAR's groundbreaking STEM Initiative, Ten80 Student Racing Challenge. The US Army shifted its sponsorship focus to scaling Ten80 Racing Challenges after recognizing their impact from working with Beverly's team as Ryan Newman's NASCAR sponsor.

Over seven years, from 2012-2019, the US Army/Ten80 Innovators in Training STEM Tour hosted over 60,000 students for one day STEM events held in 10-12 cities annually, scaling the Ten80 National STEM League.

Recognized by President Obama's 'Change the Equation' initiative as Exemplary STEM initiatives ready for broad implementation, the Ten80 Student Racing Challenges and three other programs garnered national acclaim within the business and education fields.

The Racing Challenge National STEM League is in its 17th year as a classroom, camp and competition for middle and high school students. There is an elementary version called Driving STEM that has improved the math scores of students in grades 3-6 for over twenty years using small radio-controlled cars and technology made for classrooms. During Covid, as students were forced to work from home and outside activities were limited with respect to using radio-controlled cars, autonomous vehicles, or drones, Ten80 Foundation renamed itself as The International STEM League (iNSL) to reflect its flagship program. Working with Beverly to lead the organization through this difficult time, Executive Director, Jeannie Ruiz, helped iNSL harness the power of Esports and Sim Racing in collaboration with iRacing.com, Eisengard.AI, and Rx5 CyberUnity, to keep students "on track" racing, collecting data and maximizing performance.

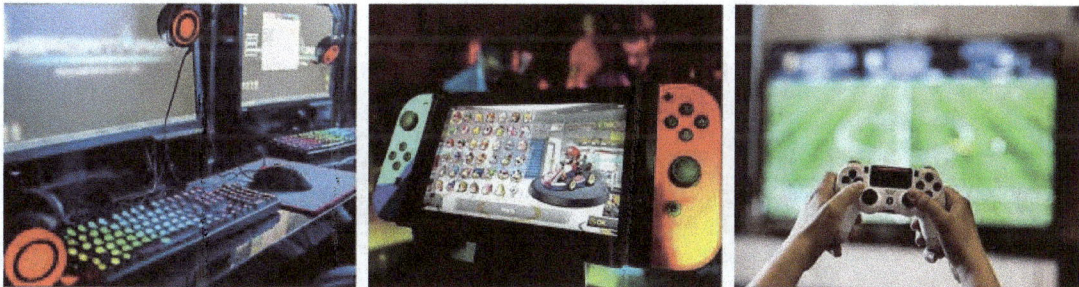

PreK - Pro Programs Engaging 1000s of Students

Beverly's accomplishments earned her a place among STEMconnector's prestigious inaugural 100 Women Leaders in STEM. Beverly also became a US State Department STEM speaker where she has provided keynotes and professional development across the US and in 8 countries.

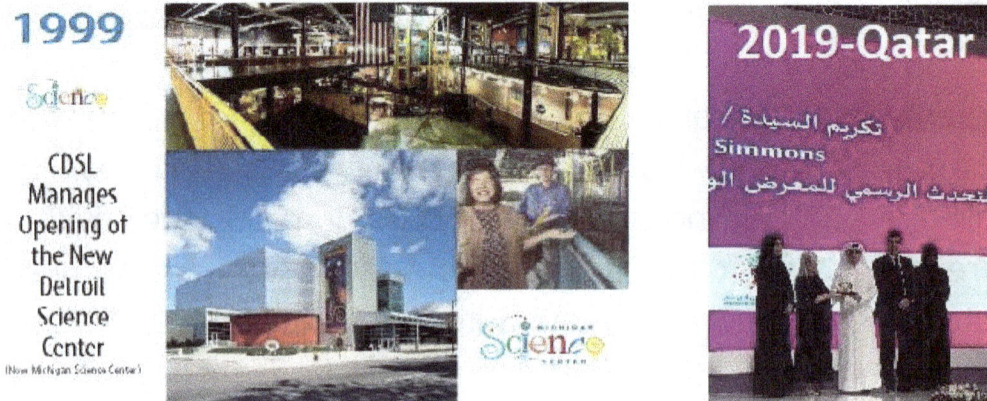

Training teachers to embrace a STEM mindset and teach it with confidence is how we can bring sySTEMic change that lasts! Beverly enjoyed raising her children and teaching other children. Now, she dedicates her time to passing on what she has learned to other teachers

Beverly Simmons

FOUNDER AND CO-CHAIR OF BOARD OF DIRECTORS TEN80 FOUNDATION

Beverly Simmons has been recognized as Teacher of the Year, GA Middle Grades Team of the Year and as a GA finalist for Presidential Awardee for Excellence in Science and Mathematics Teaching. Her informal science experience includes Spirit of Ford Conference Center, and the NEW Detroit Science Center. Simmons is Co-founder of Ten80 Education and currently serves as Founder and Co-Chair of Ten80 Foundation Board of Directors. Programs developed through her work with Ten80 include the Ten80 Student Racing Challenge: NASCAR STEM Initiative, a version of which has recently partnered with the US Army.

I. Igniting the Spark
Empower Educators to Unleash the Power of STEM

As we step into a future propelled by technology and innovation, the significance of STEM education grows ever more profound. STEM, an acronym for science, technology, engineering, and mathematics, forms the bedrock for equipping students with the necessary skills to thrive in today's workforce and the ability to thrive in the unpredictable workforce of the future.

Jobs in STEM fields are in high demand, and they offer some of the highest-paying and most exciting career opportunities available. However, many jobs will be created in the next decade that do not even exist today; Therefore, STEM skills must be presented to students in ways that teach them more than a list of algorithms in math or facts in science. While these core skills are necessary, their true value lies in the fact that they are the starting grid for creativity and innovation. Encourage students to cultivate a STEM mindset, fostering curiosity, questioning, and creative thinking, instead of solely seeking the "correct answer." Teachers should embrace lessons and activities that may not always have a definitive "key" to solutions, promoting a comfortable learning environment.

STEM skills are essential for success in all areas of modern life, and they are particularly important for students who are interested in pursuing careers in science, technology, engineering, or mathematics.
As we move into a world that is increasingly driven by fast-paced innovations in technology, it is becoming more important than ever before for students to have a strong foundation in STEM subjects. The emergence of Artificial Intelligence is not a surprise. However, few people not in the IT field expected it to make such an accessible and dramatic entry into daily life as it has in recent months. This should serve as a wake-up call to educators that we must start infusing the STEM

mindset into all classrooms to better serve the students in our care. Too many students find that they are ill-equipped to choose a career when they enter college. Their pathway is often blocked by their level of comfort and expertise in mathematics. By providing students with a strong foundation in science, technology, engineering, and mathematics, teachers can help to build the skills and mindset that students need to be in a position to have more options and opportunities with respect to their careers.

What Does it Mean to Teach STEM with Confidence?

This series of articles is based on the author's recently published book, Teaching STEM with Confidence: Practical Tips and Strategies for New and Experienced Teachers, a guide that provides practical advice and strategies for teachers to confidently integrate STEM into any subject classroom. The book is designed for both new and experienced teachers who are looking for effective and practical ways to feel confident teaching STEM.

II. What is STEM?

STEM education refers to an interdisciplinary approach to teaching science, technology, engineering, and mathematics in an integrated and cohesive manner. It aims to develop critical thinking, problem-solving, and collaboration skills while encouraging creativity, innovation, and curiosity among students. STEM education is essential in today's world as it prepares students for the challenges of the 21st century and provides them with the necessary skills to succeed in the workforce. STEM education is not only about teaching these four subjects individually. It is about integrating them into a single learning experience.

The National Science Foundation (NSF) began using the term "STEM" to refer to science, technology, engineering, and mathematics in its reports and publications in the early 2000s. The exact date of its initial usage by the NSF may vary, but it was during this time that the term gained traction and recognition within the educational and research community. The NSF has been a strong advocate for STEM education and has played a significant role in promoting and funding STEM initiatives in the United States. For example, a project that involves building an autonomous vehicle or a robot requires knowledge of various STEM concepts such as programming, mechanical engineering, and electronics. By integrating these concepts, students can see the connections between them and how they work together to achieve a common goal.

In STEM education, teachers encourage students to explore and experiment with new ideas and concepts. They also help students develop a growth mindset, which is essential in STEM fields. A growth mindset means that students believe that their intelligence and abilities can be developed through hard work, dedication, and perseverance. This mindset is critical in STEM fields as it encourages students to take risks, learn from their mistakes, and persist in the face of challenges. STEM education is not only beneficial for students but also for teachers. It provides teachers with an opportunity to collaborate and learn from each other. STEM education is a relatively new field, and there is always something new to learn.

As recently as 2012, only a decade ago, teachers attending the National Science Teachers Convention were learning about STEM. At this convention, groups of teachers came by booths with the word STEM in their company or program titles because their administrators had told them to bring back something "STEM" related. The questions they asked ranged from, "What does that even mean?" to "Do you have any STEM furniture?" and "I was told to bring something STEM back. Help?"

What, then, is the first step in this journey? Educators, many never having been exposed to the inner workings of careers outside of academia, can start by becoming comfortable with an idea that drives innovation in industry: "Fail fast, fail often." The underlying idea behind "fail fast, fail often" is that failure is not something to be feared or avoided but rather embraced and used as a stepping stone towards improvement and innovation. It encourages a mindset of resilience, adaptability, and continuous learning, fostering an environment where experimentation and creativity can thrive.

While a "STEM" class is often an exceptionally good class for students taught by an imaginative STEM literate person, it is not the embodiment of what STEM should be in our schools.

Reflections: Across the Curriculum

Some of you may remember a movement known as "Reading Across the Curriculum" that acknowledged the importance of reading as a fundamental skill that is applicable and beneficial across different disciplines. It facilitated the integration of reading skills and literacy development across various academic subjects beyond just English/language arts classes. English/language arts classes. Integrating a STEM mindset across the curriculum can help students develop critical thinking, problem-solving, and collaboration skills, which are essential for success in any field.

When I taught middle school, I always reminded myself how surprised I was on the day that I realized my students could not set up a simple graph. I walked immediately to our math teacher's room to say we had to do something differently. Jackie was also astonished because her walls were covered in graphs like the ones our students could not create in my science classroom. We will revisit this because it was my first real lesson on what it means to generalize learning.

Embrace the Role of STEM in a Country of Innovators!

America's ability to innovate is what other countries are trying to emulate. STEM skills and mindset are at the heart of innovation. Our team uses an image we created and named the STEM Innovation Arrow to drive curriculum toward STEM pathways. We will revisit it later in the book but the first thing to notice is that content and skills are at the core of innovation.

America's ability to innovate is what other countries are trying to emulate. STEM skills and mindset are at the heart of innovation. Our team uses an image we created and named the STEM Innovation Arrow to drive curriculum toward STEM pathways. We will revisit it later in the book but the first thing to notice is that content and skills are at the core of innovation.

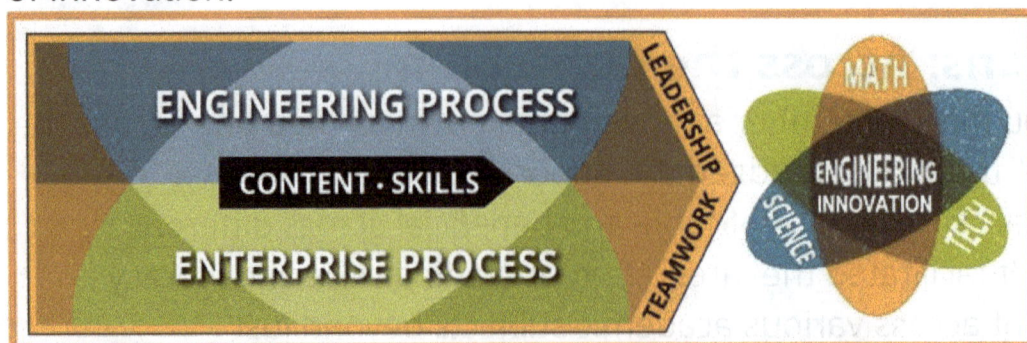

Innovation thrives when a critical mass of individuals come together in close proximity, whether physically or through virtual collaboration, to tackle shared or similar challenges. Singular contributions do not singularly birth innovations into the world. Sustaining a nation's innovative prowess in the contemporary landscape necessitates a consistent influx of individuals equipped with a foundational educational toolkit rooted in science, technology, engineering, and math (STEM) skills. This collective cohort should mirror the cultural and ideational diversity inherent within their society. Notably, a key factor in America's role as an innovation vanguard stems from the rich diversity permeating our populace.

Women and minorities are traditionally underrepresented in STEM.
STEM Education plays a pivotal role in bridging the gender and underrepresented minority gaps in K-12 achievement.
Despite accounting for around half of the employed US workforce, in 2023, the gender gap in STEM remains significant, with women making up only 28% of the STEM workforce. Only 24% of the STEM workforce are members of underrepresented minority groups. By encouraging students from diverse backgrounds to pursue STEM careers, we can create a more inclusive workforce, which will benefit society.

Too often, career-focused studies are relegated to Career Technology Education (CTE) classrooms which use a set of career pathways to prepare students for further education or post-secondary jobs. While CTE plays an important role in overall STEM education, it falls in the category of "necessary, but not sufficient".

Anyone listening to the news or social media has heard the term "labor shortage." More accurately, America is experiencing a "skills mismatch" where there is a discrepancy between the skills and qualifications possessed by job seekers and the skills demanded by employers in an ever-changing and technology-driven labor market.

Addressing this skills mismatch which can have negative consequences for both job seekers and employers requires a combination of efforts from educational institutions, employers, and policymakers. This includes aligning curriculum with industry needs, offering training and apprenticeship programs, promoting lifelong learning, and fostering effective collaboration between educational institutions and businesses.

A Hechinger Report/Associated Press analysis of CTE enrollment data from forty states reveals deep racial disparities in who takes these career-oriented courses. Black and Latino students were often less likely than their white peers to enroll in science, technology, engineering, and math (STEM) and information technology classes, according to the analysis, which was based primarily on 2017-18 data.

Meanwhile, they were more likely to enroll in courses in hospitality and, in the case of Black students in particular, human services. The median annual salary for cooks is $27,500 annually, while chefs and head cooks earn $56,000, according to the Bureau of Labor Statistics. Meanwhile, the typical engineer makes $100,000. For computer programmers, annual earnings are $92,000.

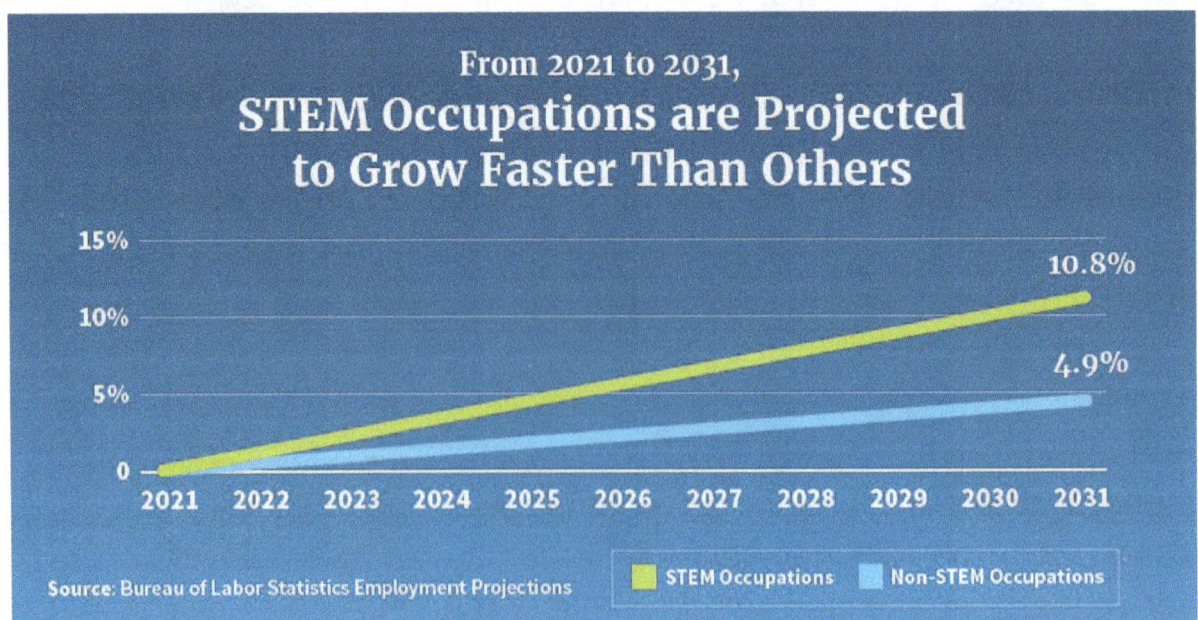

From 2021 to 2031,
STEM Occupations are Projected to Grow Faster Than Others

Source: Bureau of Labor Statistics Employment Projections

STEM Occupations — Non-STEM Occupations

Michael Dawson, who runs Innovators for Purpose, an after school STEM program based in Cambridge, Massachusetts, said schools do not do enough to expose students to different careers or nurture those with a passion in STEM. One of his former students, who loved math and science, was placed in carpentry classes, Dawson said. "I'm not sure if there's a lot of people that are really guiding these students into the types of classes that they really need to get to," Dawson said. "The counselors are busy."

Nationwide, counselors serve an average of 430 students each. At this moment, in my Vancouver WA home district, educators are striking and some of the major issues include the need for more planning time, emotional support staff, and counselors to manage the needs of students which have multiplied in complexity since COVID-19.

Across K-12 classrooms, it is imperative to harness every teaching environment—going beyond solely CTE or STEM classrooms—to ensure that the skills imparted hold real-life relevance for students and possess applicability for holistic problem-solving. STEM education serves as a conduit for instructing students in systematic and rational problem-solving approaches, equipping them with the ability to employ data-driven and evidence-based reasoning to surmount intricate challenges.

The acquisition of STEM skills confers an advantage adaptable to any forthcoming career trajectory. Conversely, an absence of these skills creates an insurmountable barrier, limiting numerous students from pursuing their desired professional paths.

Teach Resilience and Growth Mindset with STEM

The concept of "Growth Mindset" was introduced by psychologist, Carol S. Dweck, in her book titled "Mindset: The New Psychology of Success."

The book was first published in 2006. In it, Dweck explores the idea that individuals can have either a fixed mindset or a growth mindset when it comes to their abilities and intelligence. Mindset became widely influential and popularized the concept of growth mindset, leading to its widespread adoption in educational and organizational settings.

Cultivating a growth mindset stands as a pivotal element in approaching the instruction of STEM subjects with confidence. A growth mindset is rooted in the conviction that intelligence and capability evolve through diligent effort, unwavering commitment, and unyielding perseverance. It stands in stark contrast to a fixed mindset, which presupposes that intelligence and aptitude are inherent and immutable traits. This shift entails not only reevaluating our conventional emphasis on attaining the "correct solution" and pursuing an "A" grade, but also expanding and reshaping these notions to promote the development of a growth mindset. Instances where a project prototype falters still yield invaluable learning encounters. The assessment should encompass more than the capacity for rote memorization and retrieval. While not novel, this concept has yet to be fully embraced in manners that truly mirror the progressive trajectories of contemporary education.

What does it look like when educators begin to encourage a growth mindset within STEM? What kind of projects lead students in this direction? What role do "real world" problems play in an effective STEM classroom?

Only a small number of our students will find themselves employed to solve complex equations. There is simply an expectation that they possess the ability to tackle such problems and discern which equations are relevant for finding solutions. Their employability often hinges on their aptitude for handling practical tasks, the results of which may not be predetermined. Instances of "real-world challenges at a professional level could encompass:

- This electric car needs batteries that last longer on each charge and are light enough to make production of this car feasible.
- We have heavy trucks and light cars and bikes riding over the same road. What combination of materials should be used to maximize the life of our roadways?
- All young people care about is good music and wi-fi in their cars. Can we make a self-driving car that has great social technology in it?
- What material is best for my baby's sleepwear?
- And, my baby is always turning over his cereal bowl. Can't someone produce a solution to that?

This list does not begin to address the challenges faced in fields like Particle Physics and Astrophysics and Meteorology. These "real world" problems are messy and require multiple kinds of expertise and technology to formulate a workable and often compromise solution. However, the optimal solution is what one seeks. Successful STEM professionals can collaborate with a team to organize such problems, isolate variables, and identify which variables are on the critical path to a successful solution. As expert analytical people, STEM professionals, understand the limits placed on them by nature and physics and can work within the constraints placed on them by budget and material properties as well. They identify creative opportunities for improvements and sometimes market-disrupting innovations along the way.

The person who can function in this high-energy, high-stress, high-expectations workplace is the one we must be educating in our classrooms today. While not everyone will have these kinds of careers, no one should be excluded because they lack STEM literacy. To equip our students with the aptitude and outlook essential for a professional setting geared towards resolving genuine challenges, educators must acquire the ability to formulate classroom predicaments that are not only solvable but also applicable.

Problems can mimic the real world, but must be manageable versions of those to be of use in a classroom. Good projects are often set up to maximize some performance relevant to opposing variables. Setting up the investigation using "Good Investigation Procedures" (GIP) and learning to coax the story from data are the objective. As these skills are learned and practiced, the problems can become "messier."

Crafting a Project-Based Learning (PBL) curriculum that is both captivating and efficacious is as demanding to mastering any art form. This endeavor demands practice and must be facilitated by an educator at ease with the principles of a growth mindset. Teaching STEM with confidence does not require that every educator becomes a curriculum developer. Every educator needs to learn to identify and facilitate lessons that are appropriate for their students.

Reflections About Excellent and Scalable Stem:

Through Ten80 and the International STEM League, I have engaged with expert STEM professionals to develop award winning curriculum. There was a learning curve over many years, and it is not something every teacher should be expected to do. When I hear that teachers are "creating curriculum" I am sorry that their time is being diverted from their real goal: teaching.

I spent three years following industry analytical people to understand the way problems are really solved in the workplace. That experience led to the formation of the International STEM League which is designed to be a practice league for future STEM professionals. It is based on how much I learned from those experiences that I did not learn in school. It is based on all the times these expert problem solvers said, "I wish I had .... when I was in school."

The US STEM Team of the US Army funded our program to expand after President Obama's evaluation initiative endorsed our programs as Excellent STEM and Ready to Scale. Only four programs nationally reached that level of endorsement.

Over six years, our "Innovators in Training" Tour reached over one thousand students each month in one-day events that led to significant positive shifts in students' perceptions of STEM's importance in their lives and future careers. The impact was measured through independent evaluations. Moreover, these experiences spurred the formation of teams engaging with ourTen80 STEM programs, classes, and competitions.

Those first students are now in their mid-twenties and are making their mark on STEM fields. Recently, iNSL, our nonprofit organization, formalized an agreement with a Cloud Technology startup, founded by a former student. This Tech CEO introduced me to another alumnus from their TN team who has a BS in mechanical engineering and a Doctor of Education (Ed.D.) in Educational Leadership. He spearheads international STEM education strategies for a 22,000-member industry association. These are just two of many alumni who are changing the ecosystem in tech for traditionally underrepresented minorities.

III: Innovation Matters

"If invention is a pebble tossed in the pond, innovation is the rippling effect that pebble causes. Someone has to toss the pebble. That's the inventor. Someone has to recognize the ripple will eventually become a wave. That's the entrepreneur."
— (Tom Grasty, PBS Idea Lab)

Innovation tends to happen when a critical mass of people are in close proximity - physically or virtually collaborating - working on the same or similar problems. In our educational systems, we often emphasize individual innovators and their "aha" moments or screams of "Eureka," celebrating their brilliance and achievements. In doing so, we frequently miss the crucial opportunity to place these moments in the broader context of their times.

It is essential to teach students that innovation is not solely the domain of the exceptional few. With rare exceptions, it results from a collaborative process influenced by the societal and intellectual currents of the era.

Industry 4.0, alternatively known as the Fourth Industrial Revolution or 4IR, represents the forefront of digitizing the manufacturing sector. Fueled by disruptive trends such as the exponential growth of data and connectivity, advanced analytics, human-machine interaction, and significant advancements in robotics, Industry 4.0 has ushered in a remarkable acceleration of technological innovation.

In this rapidly evolving technological landscape, the pace of innovation is unparalleled. What once took years to develop now unfolds in mere weeks, reshaping not only the digital realm but also the physical world. Yet, the journey from idea to realization within this swift current is far from simple. Contrast this with the past, where technological change advanced at a glacial pace, and the technologies our ancestors embraced in their youth remained central throughout their lifetimes.

Today, educators must equip students for success in a 21st-century workplace marked by extraordinary technological velocity. This demands a willingness from teachers and administrators to adopt fresh teaching methods and innovative curricula.

With nearly 1.35 million tech startups worldwide, a staggering global internet penetration rate of 63% as of 2022, and an anticipated 463 exabytes of data production by 2025, we witness an exponential rise in connectivity and information exchange. With approximately 5 billion internet users and their numbers continually surging, the dynamics of innovation have shifted from solitary brilliance to the collective efforts of a global community. (Amardeep Pundir, 2023)

In this era, the transformative power of technology is not limited to the few but is accessible to those willing to collaborate, adapt, and contribute to the accelerating wave of progress. We have seen the power of collaboration in driving innovation since the beginning of the Scientific Revolution.

Unfolding primarily in Europe during the late 1500s and 1600s, this was a period of profound transformation in our understanding of the natural world, and stands as an early testament to the power of collaboration. It marked a seismic shift in human understanding. Scientific inquiry challenged long-held religious beliefs, moral principles, and the traditional scheme of nature. This period of questioning and discovery was facilitated by the collaborative efforts of scientists, mathematicians, and thinkers from various disciplines.

Optics, the study of light and its properties, provides one of many compelling examples of how collaboration fueled innovation during the Scientific Revolution. The work done in optics during this period laid the foundation for our modern understanding of light, vision, and the behavior of electromagnetic waves.

Scientists like Johannes Kepler, René Descartes, and Isaac Newton made significant contributions. Kepler's work on the optics of lenses, Descartes' development of the law of reflection, and Newton's groundbreaking experiments with prisms all built upon each other's ideas. Individually, these scientists were not prone to collaborative efforts. However, their society was changing due to technologies such as the printing press.

Another key element that facilitated collaboration during the Scientific Revolution was the establishment of scientific societies. These organizations were created to discuss, validate, and disseminate new discoveries. Scientific societies brought together scholars, thinkers, and practitioners, fostering an environment of shared knowledge and collaboration.

Scientific papers emerged as vital tools for communicating complex ideas comprehensibly. They allowed scientists to share their discoveries, hypotheses, and methodologies with their peers. The newly emerging scientific method allowed scientists to test and verify the conclusions of their peers. Shared papers underwent rigorous scrutiny, which encouraged further refinement of ideas and experiments. This collaborative approach accelerated the progress of science and the development of ever improved technologies.

The influence of scientific collaborations during the Scientific Revolution extended beyond the realm of science and directly impacted all areas of society, such as art. One fascinating example is the connection between the renowned Dutch painter Johannes Vermeer and the scientific instrument known as the camera obscura. Vermeer's work serves as a striking testament to the interplay between art and science during this transformative period.

The camera obscura, which translates to "dark chamber" in Latin, is an optical device that projects an image of the external world onto a surface inside a darkened room. During the Scientific Revolution, the camera obscura was not just a scientific curiosity. It also became a tool for artists and curious minds. It allowed for the accurate depiction of perspective, proportion, and light in ways that were previously challenging to achieve. Vermeer, like many artists of his time, is believed to have used the camera obscura to aid in his artistic process.

Vermeer's paintings are renowned for their exquisite rendering of light and its interplay with objects and spaces. The camera obscura can produce a focused image with depth, similar to how Vermeer's works often have a sense of depth and focal accuracy. The camera obscura can create soft-focus areas and smooth gradations often seen in Vermeer's artworks. This mastery of light in his works aligns closely with the principles of optics and the scientific understanding of light emerging during the Scientific Revolution.

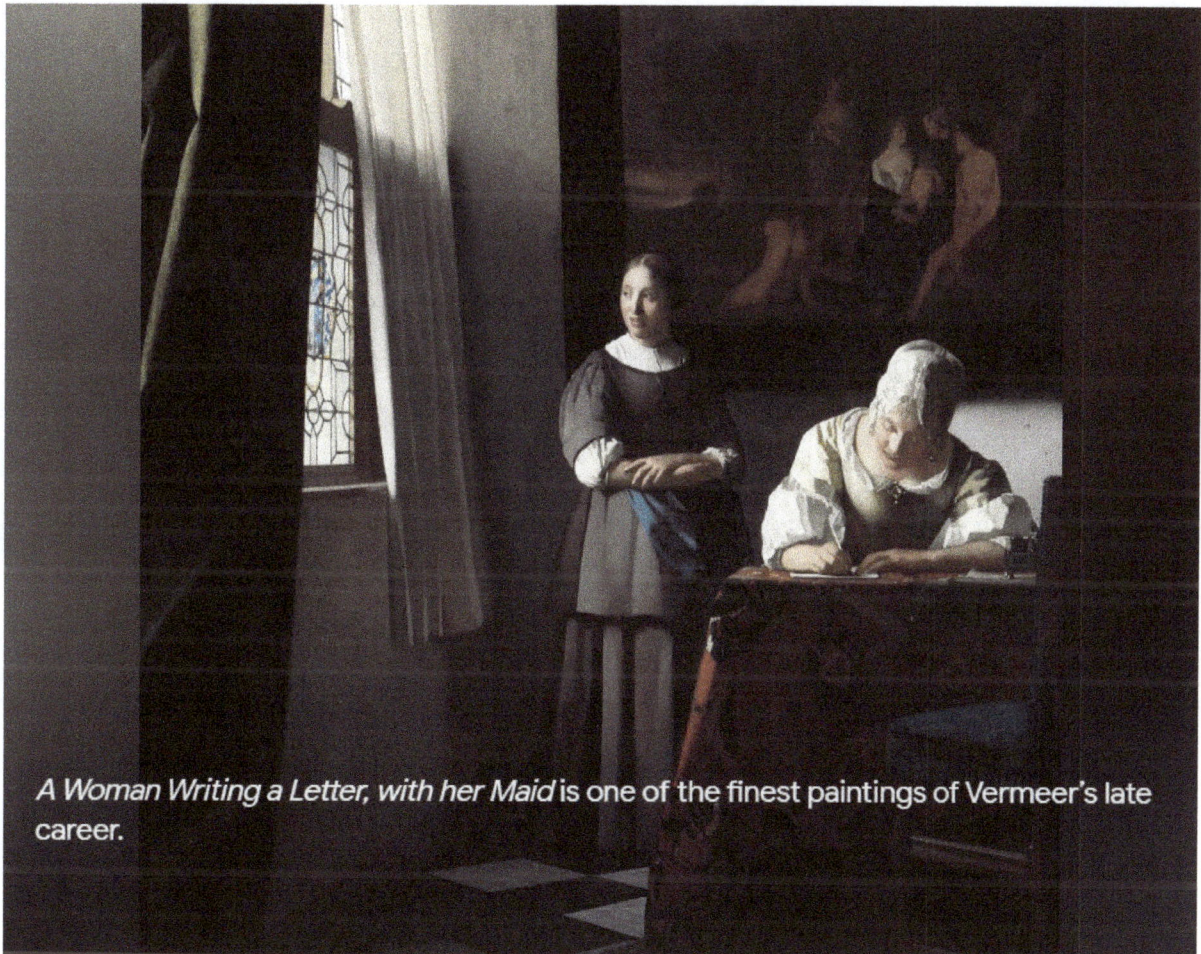

A Woman Writing a Letter, with her Maid is one of the finest paintings of Vermeer's late career.

The story of Johannes Vermeer and his use of the camera obscura serves as a compelling example of how scientific collaborations and innovations influence every facet of society. Vermeer's ability to capture light and perspective in his paintings was enhanced by his engagement with the scientific discoveries of his era.

this story underscores the idea that during times of great intellectual ferment, boundaries between disciplines blur, leading to a rich cross-pollination of ideas and creativity.

It is clear that such connections are happening in our world today. Young artists are often more adept at drawing with digital software than a pencil, marker, or charcoal. Ai is helping graphic arts take great leaps in what can be created and altered. Movies are often created by actors in front of green screens using CGI.

Innovation today is not limited to one industry or one facet of society. The connected world is one in which we are living and one in which we must, as educators, thrive if we are to confidently lead our students to succeed in this high-tech workplace.

The speed of technological innovations in the 21st century owes much to the rapid communication enabled by the worldwide internet system. Scientists and mathematicians from around the globe can now collaborate in real time, 24/7.

While concerns about secrecy within organizations persist, the benefits of having more minds working on a problem far outweigh the drawbacks. The internet has become the modern equivalent of the scientific societies of the past, connecting experts and enabling collaborative problem-solving.

STEM Ecosystems have grown across the country in the past few years as educators attempt to support one another's understanding and supplement one another's resources in much the same way as the scientific community has done since the Scientific Revolution began. As STEM teachers, we should also engage students intrigued by the intersection of art and science, sometimes called STEAM. As novel techniques, software, and technologies emerge regularly, the dynamic interplay between art and science undergoes constant and evolving transformations. We should teach about these intersections of subjects and society so that learning is less siloed. It is not enough to know the names and a few facts about early scientists. It does not help one understand how early innovations actually happened and it fosters the belief in students that scientist are all white men with wild hair. The idea that only a select few are smart enough to be innovative is an idea that is not appropriate for modern times.

Innovation is what makes America a country to be envied and emulated. All students can be part of that today if they understand the role that technology can play to even playing fields. It is imperative that we, as educators, stay informed and knowledgeable about this ever-changing landscape and work to grow our own collaborative network of like-minded STEM focused teachers.

The International STEM League (iNSL) is pioneering an award-winning approach to STEM education that views it as a "performing art" demanding practice, dedication, and enthusiasm. We believe that being innovative is not just about what you know but about forging new paths, shifting perspectives, and envisioning transformative solutions. It is a thought process cultivated from our earliest experiences, where imagination takes root. The richness of these neural pathways, fostered through interdisciplinary learning, not only reinforces concepts but also cultivates creativity, critical thinking, and problem-solving skills.

Rather than compartmentalizing knowledge and skills, an integrated approach connects STEM subjects within a relevant context, aligning with real-world applications. We understand that educators should have the flexibility to customize and adapt STEM programs to their students' unique learning styles and needs. We advocate for teachers to be equipped with the tools and insights necessary to unveil the evolution of big ideas in science and technology, reinforcing the relevance of their teachings.

By instilling STEM awareness and a project-based learning mindset, teachers can spark systemic change in education, nurturing the creative and innovative thinking essential for our students to thrive in an ever-evolving world. In the end, It is not just about imparting knowledge; It is about empowering our future "Innovators in Training" to shape a brighter tomorrow through the dynamic world of STEM.

Reflections – Camera Obscura

Lesson Overview
Materials needed per student or pair of students:

- Empty Pringles can (or similar can, like an oatmeal can)
- push pin
- 1 foot of aluminum foil
- scissors
- tape
- waxed paper or tracing paper

I recommend this as one of many great lessons on making camera obscuras.

https://annex.exploratorium.edu/science-explorer/pringles_pinhole.html

Reflections – Where's the Math?

In 1995, pre-digital cameras, a visiting engineer, helped me and my students have our first interaction with integrated STEM projects. We used a video camera to record students dropping egg carriers from an 8-foot ladder. We created a release mechanism to control the drops and placed a tape with measurements on the wall behind the drop area. The last step was to use a stop frame VCR (look it up:) to play back the videos on the classroom TV with a clear acetate sheet on the TV surface. When each video started, students used a Sharpie to mark the position of the egg carrier on the acetate.

The video played at 30 frames per second, so we stopped it every three frames and marked where the carrier was after one-tenth of a second. We could all SEE that the carrier dropped a greater distance with each tenth of a second than in the previous tenth of seconds.

For the first time, my students SAW acceleration, the speed change due to gravity's pull. Things fall farther in the same time as gravity accelerates the object. Later, we would drop things from the ladder on the local fire truck and SEE what terminal velocity meant as dropped items stopped accelerating. Because we had a tape measure in the background, we could tell how far it fell in each tenth second. We could see how the activity of the carrier's parachute reacted during the fall and map it to the speed and acceleration of the carrier.

When students graphed the data and compared carrier designs, they made their first data-driven decisions. They won the state competition for three years in a row. By the third year, they were shocked that the other schools never seemed to have any numbers to support their designs.

This lesson today can be taught using digital cameras and counting frames is much simplified. It can also be taught with online simulators from groups like Phet. However, there is a worthwhile learning experience in having students see the egg crate they built on the screen, marking its acceleration on top of it, and internalizing that experience with both their hands and their minds

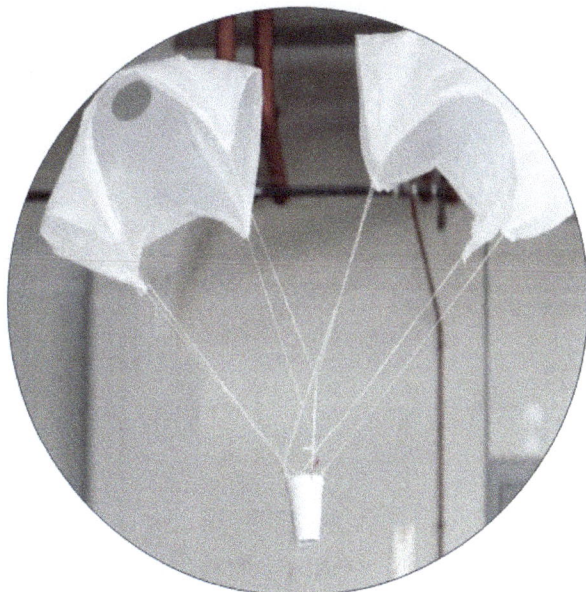

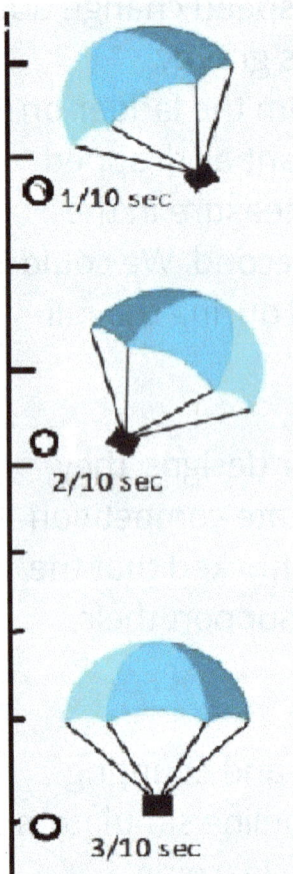

1/10 sec

2/10 sec

3/10 sec

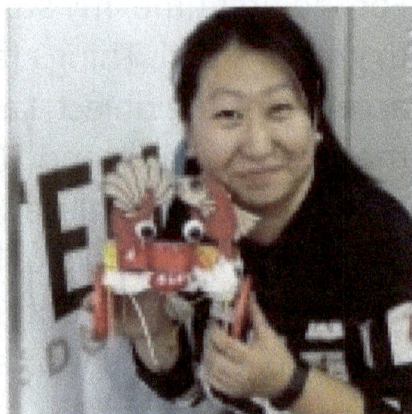

IV. 5 Simple Pieces
Foster Innovation in the Classroom

1. **Emphasize effort over talent**
   When giving feedback to your students, focus on their effort rather than their innate ability. Encourage them to embrace challenges and view mistakes as opportunities for growth.

2. **Teach the power of "yet".**
   When a student says, "I can't do this," remind them to add the word "yet" at the end. This simple addition changes the statement from a fixed mindset to a growth mindset and encourages students to keep working towards their goals.

3. **Use growth mindset language**
   Be mindful of the language you use when talking to your students. Avoid phrases like "you're so smart" or "you're a natural at this." Instead, use language that emphasizes effort and growth, such as "I can see you worked really hard on this" or "I'm proud of you for persevering through this challenge."

4. **Provide opportunities for growth**
   Give your students opportunities to challenge themselves and learn new things. Encourage them to take on projects that are outside their comfort zone and provide support and guidance as they work through the challenges

5. **Model a growth mindset**
   Finally, be a role model for your students by demonstrating a growth mindset in your own work. Share your own challenges and mistakes with your students and talk about how you overcame them through hard work and perseverance.

By developing a growth mindset in our STEM students, we can help them become confident, resilient learners who are ready to tackle any challenge that comes their way. STEM education is a term that has gained widespread popularity in recent years, and with good reason. It is an approach to teaching and learning that focuses on the integration of science, technology, engineering, and mathematics (STEM) in a way that promotes critical thinking, problem solving, and creativity. As educators, it is essential that we understand the basics of STEM so that we can effectively teach and inspire our students.

The first step in understanding STEM is to recognize that it is more than just a collection of subjects. STEM is an interdisciplinary approach that emphasizes the integration of knowledge from different fields. This means that instead of thinking of science, technology, engineering, and mathematics as separate subjects, we should teach them as interconnected and interdependent disciplines. While each field possesses fundamental knowledge which must be taught, this knowledge alone is inadequate for achieving success in any career path other than the theoretical.

How do these subjects intersect with one another?
Teaching the Basics with a STEM

Science is about real, tangible things that move, fly, explode, burn, haul loads, float, record images, stop diseases, and explore the universe. It includes all the interesting exciting "creations" of the times in which we live. Science and mathematics have a symbiotic relationship.

Mathematics provides the language and tools for expressing scientific concepts and theories quantitatively. It helps scientists analyze data, formulate hypotheses, create models, and make predictions. Conversely, science provides real-world contexts and applications that inspire and drive mathematical investigations. The empirical observations and experiments of science often require mathematical reasoning and analysis for interpretation and understanding.

Engineering and Technology share a close relationship as well. Technology encompasses the practical application of scientific knowledge and engineering principles to create useful products, processes, or systems. Engineers utilize technology to design, develop, and optimize solutions for real-world problems. Technology, in turn, informs and supports engineering practices by providing tools, materials, and techniques. Engineering focuses on problem-solving, applying scientific and mathematical principles to design and build structures, devices, and systems that meet specific needs and goals.

Mathematics plays a crucial role in engineering. Engineers use mathematical principles and calculations to analyze, model, and optimize designs. Mathematics provides the foundation for engineering concepts like calculus, differential equations, statistics, and linear algebra. Engineers rely on mathematical tools and models to quantify and predict system behavior, assess feasibility, and ensure safety and efficiency.

Science, mathematics, technology, and engineering are interconnected disciplines that leverage each other's strengths to advance knowledge, solve problems, and drive innovation. The integration of these disciplines through Many of us remember how separated the core subjects were from each other in the not too distant past. In 2004, less than 20 years ago, a team of presenters from my emerging professional development company traveled to a different rural school in GA each day to present model lessons.

We called the program Math2Go and it was all about having kids and teachers Newton's three laws. I received a call when this team was refused entry to the classroom because the teacher proclaimed that she did not need math lessons in her science classroom.

Teachers are not being asked to teach an additional subject in an already crowded curriculum. They are tasked with recognizing the interdisciplinary nature of STEM, incorporating it across the curriculum, emphasizing hands on learning, promoting problem-solving, and encouraging creativity. Together, educators in a grade level or a school can create a learning environment that embraces STEM literacy for all students.

Planning a Lesson - Just the Basics

Planning an effective learning experience, a lesson, is a skill all effective teachers master. It can seem daunting at first, especially for new teachers who are just starting out in their teaching career. However, with the right tools and strategies, it can be a rewarding and fulfilling experience for both the teacher and the student. In this chapter, we will explore some Lesson planning starts with identifying the learning objectives.
What do you want your students to learn? What skills do you want them to develop? What is the expected outcome? How will the learned skill or objective generalize to broader understanding. Once you have identified the learning objectives and many districts or schools take this step for teachers, it is time to start to design your lesson plan.

The next step is to choose the right activities and resources.
STEM education is all about applied and often, hands-on learning, so it is important to choose activities that will engage your students and allow them to explore and discover new concepts while practicing the core skills for which you are responsible as a grade level teacher. You can choose from a wide range of resources, including online simulations, interactive games, and physical materials like building blocks and circuit boards. When designing your lesson plan, take the opportunity to consider the different learning styles of your students.

While the effectiveness of tailoring instruction to specific learning styles is still a topic of debate, some research suggests that instructional approaches that incorporate a variety of modalities and cater to diverse learning preferences can benefit all learners.

STEM education also emphasizes the importance of problem-solving through data. Including data collection and analysis in a lesson is a simple step that can help teachers avoid the significant pitfall of many STEM programs, especially those for younger grades. Programs only address the S, the T, and the E; the math is considered optional. When STEM became a sellable commodity, many science lessons were suddenly labeled STEM. This was done by large and small developers and helped create many problems in implementation of effective STEM practices.

In several states over the past decade, when administrators at the state level or in the University system created STEM standards, they made arbitrary rules such as needing to include at least two or three of the STEM subjects in the lesson for it to qualify as STEM.

In one state, the Eastern half required two subjects and the Western half decided to require three to differentiate their research and grant platforms. This is not a useful or meaningful way to define STEM learning.

Another fundamental aspect of STEM education is the importance of Project Based Learning. STEM subjects are best taught through hands-on experiences that allow students to engage, explore, experiment, explain, and extend learning. Making data driven decisions and conclusions is an important part of this process because a poorly designed lesson can waste a lot of time with hands-on but not minds-on learning. Poor planning can miss a multitude of opportunities.

Imagine a scenario where a science teacher seamlessly integrates scale lessons and scientific notation into her curriculum, when covering a wide array of subjects such as cells, planets, elements, animals, and speed. Coinciding with this, the math teacher is delving into exponents and decimals. This synchronicity in teaching not only imparts valuable skills to students but also offers them a platform to apply those skills. By engaging in daily exercises, or bell ringers, in both classes that involve gauging the magnitude of various attributes like size, speed, weight, area, volume, and density, students establish a foundation for essential benchmarks. These benchmarks, in turn, equip them to make estimations and identify mathematically nonsensical outcomes with confidence, thus enhancing their comprehension within the realm of mathematics.

Well-designed projects can involve anything from building an autonomously driving vehicle from an off-the-shelf radio-controlled car to creating a functioning robot to designing experiments in a laboratory. Recently the International STEM League projects have evolved with the addition of Esports blending hands-on learning with gaming to teach a number of physics concepts.

By engaging in hands-on, project-based activities, evidence has shown that students are more likely to retain what they learn and develop a deeper understanding of the subject matter.

This is not a new idea and there is a large research base available. An early study in Canada provides a good summary of the positive outcomes of this kind of learning: The Impact of Hands-On-Approach on Student Academic Performance in Basic Science and Mathematics *(Cecilia O. Ekwueme1 , Esther E. Ekon1 & Dorothy C. Ezenwa-Nebife, 2015) and The Effect of Active Learning Techniques on Academic Performance and Learning Retention in Science Lesson: An Experimental Study, Aykan, A. ., & Dursun, F. (2022). Vol. 2 No. 1 (2022): The Journal of STEM Teacher Institutes)*

More updated research is available through sites like the Journal of STEM Teacher Institutes. One new study and strategic plan published in NC by EdNC, "A vision for STEM education over the next decade," highlights project-based learning and problem-based learning as two promising instructional strategies that develop these skills:

"Through project-based learning, a well-established practice, students gain knowledge and skills by working for an extended period to investigate and respond to complex questions, problems, or challenges relevant to students' experiences and communities. Students engage in the work with careful support and guidance from teachers. Students learn and practice such skills as calculating acceleration and writing persuasively within the context of a substantive six-to-eight weeks project."

Failure is a bump in the road to success! Get Creative!

In the realm of STEM education, one crucial aspect is the significance of creativity. Recently, a LinkedIn group was formed to explore whether teachers think students are more creative today.

My thought was that students have always been creative, but now schools are more accepting of learning styles that foster creativity rather than stifle it. STEM disciplines go beyond rigid rule-following; they inherently demand a spark of creativity and a spirit of innovation. Encouraging students to transcend boundaries and think beyond the conventional, STEM education fosters the cultivation of fresh perspectives and the pursuit of inventive solutions to challenges. It celebrates the power of thinking "outside the box," encouraging learners to embrace their creative potential in shaping a future fueled by imagination and ingenuity.

The four main learning styles are visual, auditory, reading/writing, and kinesthetic. Some students may learn better through visual aids, while others may prefer hands-on activities. One style really does not fit all. By incorporating a variety of teaching methods into your lesson plan and using multiple representations to introduce new concepts, you can ensure that all of your students are engaged and learning.

When I taught my first workshop in China, our team was not expecting to be critiqued by our adult students until the end of the workshop. At the end of the first day, at their request, our team met with their lead teachers to reflect on the day and get their feedback on how well we met their needs, any questions they noted, and suggestions we might incorporate the next day. It was an extremely helpful, if somewhat intimidating, interaction that our team learned from and uses today. This communication also led us to watch closely how they interacted with one another during activities.

Asian teachers are incredibly open and sharing within their groups. They would compare how one group introduces a concept, demonstrate it, invite critiques, and then compare it to how another group introduces the same topic. The critiques left them with multiple ways to represent a concept to their students and helped individuals identify misconceptions.

Teachers must strive to provide opportunities for students to work collaboratively. STEM education emphasizes teamwork and problem-solving, so it is important to create a classroom environment that fosters cooperation and communication. You can do this by assigning group projects or encouraging students to work together on individual assignments.

Finally, it is important to assess your students' learning throughout the lesson. This can be done through formative assessments, such as quizzes and group discussions, as well as summative assessments, such as exams and projects. For project assessments, having a rubric allows students to self-assess as they progress through the project. It is also a template for feedback and grades given to the students. By regularly assessing students' progress, you can ensure through data that they are mastering the concepts and skills that you are teaching.

K-12 STEM Education is an opportunity to help students begin to connect the conceptual dots learned in all the traditional subjects including art and the humanities. It should offer educators concrete and clear opportunities to collaborate and reinforce ideas across subjects.

The problems with which students are taught cannot be as messy as the ones solved in industry. Classroom problems should be small enough to be investigated with quantifiable outcomes. They often have opposing variables: if one condition improves, another declines. They are often about maximization and may not have a right or wrong answer but one that depends on the conditions in which the test is run. Students need to be encouraged to identify and control variables. This is the beginning of learning to solve problems that are real world messy.

Here is an example of how project-based hands-on learning might look.

Create a project in which students collect data while teams drive radio-controlled cars with different weights taped onto the cars during a class or after school. Students are attempting to determine at what weight their vehicle is getting maximum efficiency. It is a Goldilocks problem with a score based on weight and speed.

One such score is (weight times distance) / average speed. Students use technology to record weight, length of the track, and elapsed time of each run in a logbook along with notes about any data that seems to be an outlier. For instance, "Marcia was not used to driving and her time was affected by that factor more than the weight of the car."

During the week, the math class uses the data to teach graphing, best fit lines, or derive linear and quadratic equations. In elementary classes, the data can be used to practice graphing and computation such as averaging times from three timers.

The graphs and math models that can be generated from this kind of investigation can be grade leveled from third through twelve by ramping up the math analysis of the data collected.

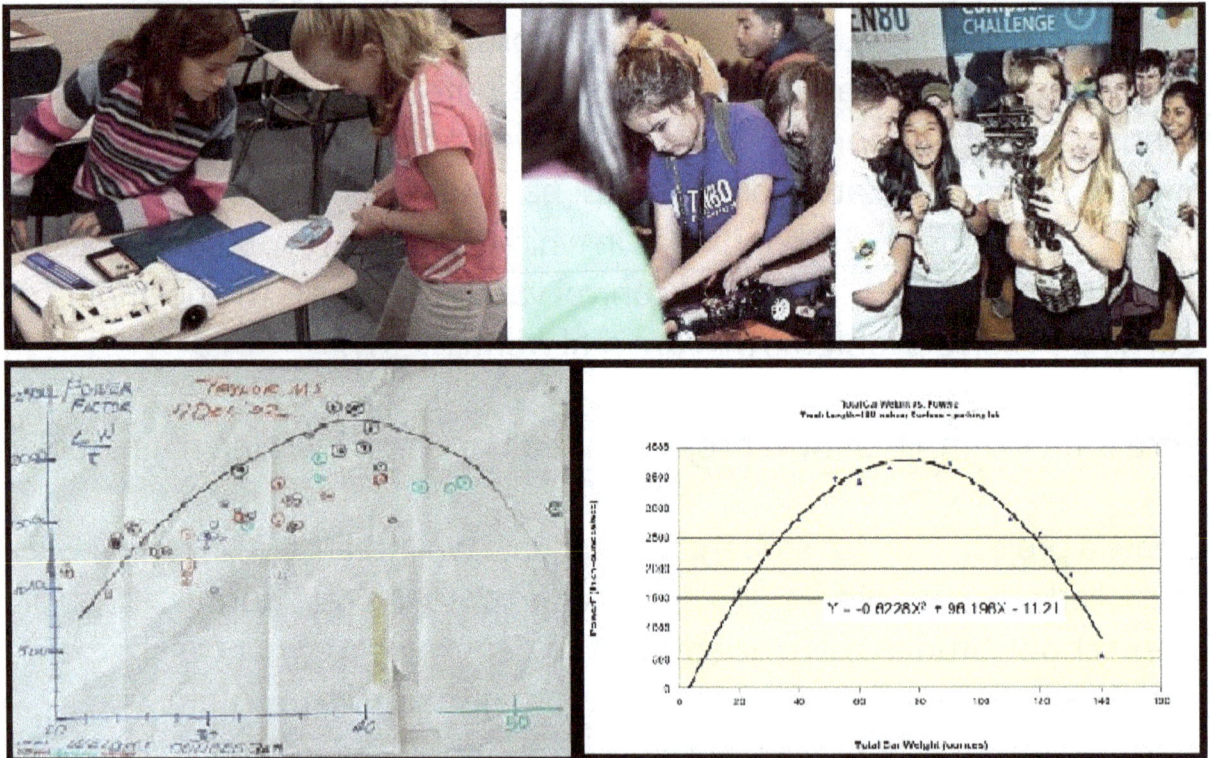

In science, the data lends itself to learning about mass and weight and Newton's laws of motion or thermodynamic, batteries, and energy depending on the objectives being taught at the time.

In CTE classes, carriers for placing weight on the car or ramps and bridges with adjustable heights for further investigation can be designed and built or online wind tunnels and CAD programs or Esports like iRacing can be used to show how digital or radio-controlled cars mimics what happens to actual vehicles. Data can also be downloaded from online iRacing for analysis.

History teachers can integrate the story of early developers of math, science, and technology used in automobiles into social studies lessons as appropriate.

The same decision-making process used in this lesson can be used to determine the maximum ticket price for a school concert. At what price point do the planners break even and at what point do student purchases begin to drop off? The process also generalizes to determining solutions in chemistry and to the concept of power and energy transfer in physics.

Though all this learning and practicing takes place, when asked what the kids did all day and all quarter, they will say they drove cars in math class every Fridays.

This example could have been about designing and prototyping a greenhouse for the school grounds. It could be about planning a garden with geometrically shaped flower beds that will attract butterflies and hummingbirds.

It is amazing how many teachers are doing great STEM lessons in the guise of projects and are simply unaware that their work is the true meaning of STEM. Others just need to think about their projects and make sure that they are tilting it toward STEM.

- Collect and Analyze Data! This is the first and simplest method for creating a STEM focus in a lesson for teachers beginning to integrate STEM into their planning. Use Good Investigative Practices (GIP). Incorporate an Engineering Design Cycle for prototypes.

- Use the Scientific Method to plan experiments. Integrate STEM into your classroom by looking at each lesson with an eye to what can be evaluated or investigated that lends itself to data collection. Any investigation uses the scientific process and any time you use data to predict how something will react or to improve its performance, you are engaging in very basic engineering design thinking.

Planning any lesson requires careful thought and preparation, but with the right tools, strategies, and mindset, it can be a rewarding and engaging experience for both you and your students.

DEFINE A PROBLEM®
Define or Redefine a Need or Problem

IMPROVE THE SOLUTION®
Integrate Feedback into an Improved Solution

IDENTIFY
Research Criteria and Constraints *(Do not re-invent the wheel)*

SHARE RESULTS®
Justify Next Move

DESIGN CYCLE

BRAINSTORM SOLUTIONS®
Come up with Possible Solutions

EVALUATE RESULTS
Appraise and Compare to Criteria and Constraints

MAKE AND TEST
The Best Solution

Reflections: Pom Pom Catapults

By identifying learning objectives, choosing the right activities and resources, catering to different learning styles, promoting teamwork, and assessing student progress, you can create a dynamic and effective lesson that will inspire and empower your students. Integrating STEM can start with something as simple as looking up or collecting data to gain more insight into what you are studying. It can be as fun as shooting pom poms!

At the end of the book, you will find an index of several lessons that may help you think about how to plan your next STEM experience.

Pom Pom Catapults is one our team uses because students from K-6 can take part in the activity and the learning objectives can range from simple counting and measurement to controlling variables and finding patterns in collected data. My hope is that you will look at objectives you must teach and think about how you can customize this activity to help students practice skills as they solve a problem.

A copy of this lesson is included at the end of the book.

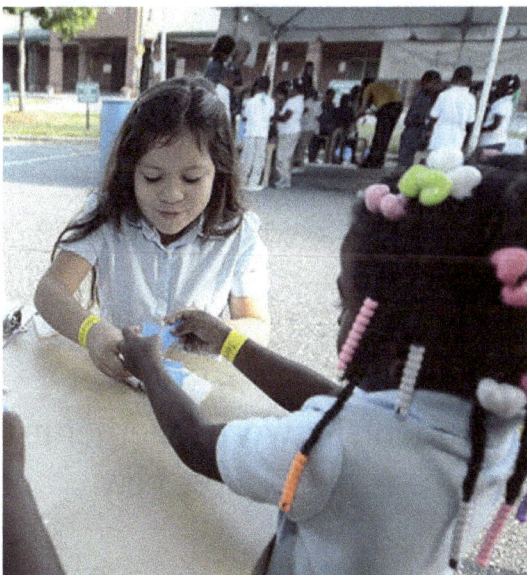

V: Creating a STEM-Friendly Classroom
Strategies for Making a STEM Focused Environment

Creating a STEM-friendly classroom is essential to encourage students to develop a strong interest in the science, technology, engineering, and mathematics fields.

As a teacher in the STEM Education niche, you need to create an atmosphere that fosters creativity, innovation, and curiosity in your students. Here are some practical tips and strategies to help you create a STEM-friendly classroom:

Tables Encourage Collaboration: One of the essential skills in STEM education is collaboration. Encourage your students to work together in small groups to solve problems, brainstorm new ideas, and explore new concepts.

Provide Hands-on Materials and Tools: STEM subjects are best learned through hands-on experiences. Let them move, touch, and measure. Provide your students with tools such as scales, stopwatches, timers, multi- meters, and tape measures as well as opportunities to conduct experiments, build models, and work with technology. This will help to keep their interest levels high and engage them in the learning process.

Make Connections to Real-World Applications: Fostering connections to real-world applications is crucial for cultivating student engagement in STEM subjects. When students can directly witness the practical implications of science, technology, engineering, and mathematics, their enthusiasm and interest are more likely to be ignited. In my classroom, I found that designing programs centered around cars and racing captured students' attention effectively. Given that most individuals possess experience with cars or transportation, and the thrill of racing adds an element of excitement, this approach proved engaging.

It is imperative to demonstrate to students how STEM disciplines empower expert problem solvers to tackle complex real-world challenges, such as climate change. Just as budding professional baseball players start their journey by honing skills in T-Ball and Little League, novice and intermediate problem solvers must enthusiastically embrace the practice of STEM skills and participation in STEM competitions. This active involvement not only paves the way for skill development but also instills a profound appreciation for the practicality and impact of STEM knowledge.

Use Technology to Enhance Learning: Technology is an essential tool in STEM education. Use it to provide your students with access to online resources, virtual field trips, and simulations. This will help to enhance their learning experience and keep them engaged. Remember, technology is not always wired. It can be scales and calculators and calipers.

Celebrate Diversity: STEM fields are traditionally male dominated. As a teacher, you need to encourage diversity and inclusion in your classroom. Celebrate the achievements of women and minorities in STEM and provide your students with role models from diverse backgrounds.

Provide opportunities for self-directed learning: STEM subjects require a lot of independent study and self-directed learning. Provide students with resources such as textbooks, online tutorials, and educational games that they can use to explore the material on their own.

Incorporate interdisciplinary learning: STEM subjects are often interrelated, and incorporating interdisciplinary learning can help students see how different subjects connect. For example, a lesson on robotics could include elements of physics, engineering, and computer science.

Creating a STEM-friendly classroom requires a combination of practical strategies and a positive attitude. Encourage collaboration, provide hands- on learning opportunities, make connections to real-world applications, use technology to enhance learning, and celebrate diversity. By doing so, you will help to develop a love of STEM in your students and prepare them for success in the future.

Incorporating Technology in STEM Lessons

Incorporating technology in STEM lessons has become increasingly important in the current education landscape. Technology has revolutionized the way we teach STEM subjects, making it possible for teachers to engage their students in a more interactive and meaningful learning experience. Again, it is important to remember that not all technology is computer or network or cloud based. While computers and digital devices are commonly associated with technology, the scope of technology extends beyond just computers.

Technology refers to the application of scientific knowledge and tools to solve problems, improve efficiency, and enhance human life. It encompasses a wide range of tools, techniques, and systems that are designed to achieve specific objectives.

Tools are instruments or devices that are created to perform specific tasks or facilitate human activities. They can be manual, mechanical, or electronic in nature. Examples of non-computer-based technology include simple hand tools like hammers, wrenches, and screwdrivers, as well as more complex machinery, equipment, and appliances used in various industries.

Incorporating digital technology in STEM lessons can be accomplished using educational apps and software. There are numerous apps and software available specifically designed for STEM education, which can be used to supplement conventional teaching methods. For instance, there are apps that allow students to simulate scientific experiments, which can be especially helpful for teaching complex concepts that are difficult to demonstrate in a traditional classroom setting.

Another way of incorporating technology in STEM lessons is with multimedia resources. With my first experience using a headset and virtual reality, I took a trip to the moon in an Apollo capsule, and I stood beside a dinosaur later the same day. It was awe inspiring and made me begin to understand how many opportunities we can give our students.

Multimedia resources such as videos, animations, and interactive graphics can be used to illustrate complex concepts and make them easier to understand. Teachers can also use multimedia resources to create interactive quizzes and assessments to evaluate students' understanding of the subject matter.

Virtual field trips are another way of incorporating technology in STEM lessons. Virtual field trips allow students to explore different environments and ecosystems without leaving the classroom. There are many virtual field trip platforms available, which offer a wide range of subjects and topics to choose from. Teachers can use these platforms to supplement their teaching and provide students with a more immersive learning experience.

Incorporating technology in STEM lessons can also involve the use of social media and other online platforms. This method is subject to safety concerns at each location. Teachers can use social media platforms such as Twitter and Facebook to share resources and engage with their students.

Online platforms such as Google Classroom can also be used to facilitate collaboration and communication between teachers and students.
In today's rapidly evolving educational landscape, educators face the imperative of embracing and integrating new technologies within their classrooms. With the advent of AI, the role of technology in education has become even more significant. Students rely on their teachers to possess awareness and updated knowledge about the ways in which emerging technologies can enhance the learning experience. I can recall an instance where a business education teacher opted for retirement, citing an inability to adapt to new tools like "excel." This underscores the importance of teachers taking personal accountability for staying abreast of changes in the professional world, as it directly impacts the students' preparation for future success.

While not every teacher needs to be a coding expert, it is essential to comprehend the essence of coding and possess resources to support students in this area. Embracing the lifelong journey of learning may be time-intensive, yet it distinguishes effective educators and instills in students a sense of confidence inspired by their teachers' commitment to growth and adaptability.

As cloud computing and generative Ai and other technologies that are confusing to many who are not in IT fields, policy makers need to make sure teachers are offered workshops to keep them up on what these technologies are even if they are not expected to use them. We must think of these challenges to be lifelong learners as exciting rather than overwhelming.

Problem-Solving Prowess with Data-Driven PBL

Project-based learning is a teaching approach that has gained popularity in recent years, especially in the field of STEM education. It involves organizing classroom activities around projects that require students to solve real-world problems or create something new.

You may notice that many of the projects highlighted in the book have to do with cars. That is because my team learned that we could inspire and engage kids with the theater of racing in grades K-12. Where does your passion overlap with a topic that lends itself to engaging kids while offering ways to explore, investigate, prototype, and do on a classroom scale what experts do in the real world.

Project-based learning is a student-centered approach to teaching that promotes critical thinking, collaboration, communication, and creativity.

In this image, you see the progression of the same basic problem of maximizing performance of radio-controlled cars PreK to Grade 12. Lessons expand each year based on grade level math and science skills.

PBL also gives students the opportunity to work on projects that are interesting and challenging, which motivates them to learn more about STEM subjects. Post COVID-19, INSL projects evolved to focus on hands-on projects designed to accompany Esports gaming.

Here are some practical tips and strategies for implementing project-based learning in STEM education:

- Start with a clear learning objective.
  Before you begin a project, make sure you have a clear learning objective in mind. This will help you identify or design a project that is aligned with your learning goals and will enable students to achieve the desired outcomes.
- Create a rubric.
  Rubrics make explicit the way in which the team and the project itself will be evaluated. This makes sure that everyone is working toward the same goal and has the same expectations.
- Choose a relevant and engaging topic.
  Select a topic that is relevant to your students' interests and experience. This will help them engage with the project and stay motivated throughout the learning process.
- Provide guidance and support.
  While project-based learning is student-centered, it is essential to provide guidance and support to students throughout the project.
- Offer feedback and constructive criticism to help them improve their work and provide resources to help them overcome challenges.
- Encourage collaboration.
  Collaboration is an essential part of project-based learning. Encourage students to work together in groups to solve problems and create

innovative solutions. Have a list of "jobs" or "roles" that need to be filled so that each team member knows what is expected of them. This will help them develop teamwork skills that are critical for success in STEM careers.

- Celebrate success.
  When the project is complete, celebrate the students' success. Display their work in the classroom or have them present it to the school community.

Celebrating success will help students feel proud of their achievements and motivated to continue learning. Some groups are creating online portfolio galleries in Metaverse form using software that is free or relatively inexpensive for a school or youth organization.

Students enjoy a gamified atmosphere and respond well to earning points for their work as it is completed and awards or certificates for completion of the project.

Reflections on "interesting and relevant."

During my tenure as the developer of The Eagle Team, an Expanded Age Group Learning Experience, I had a transformative experience that underscores the effectiveness of project-based learning. This narrative serves as a testament to convince educators that this approach can effectively meet objectives while fostering student ownership of their work.

In my last three years as a science teacher, I was part of a four-member team instructing middle grades in a standard 800-student Georgia middle school. Our wing was granted the opportunity to experiment with a multi-age classroom concept, and we collectively taught 120 students: forty each from sixth, seventh, and eighth grades. Although those three years could fill a book on their own, it is pertinent to highlight a specific incident during the third year, which coincided with my nomination for an award.

Unexpectedly, an evaluation team from GA Tech and UGA visited my classroom. Gathered around a table as the bell rang, we observed thirty students entering the room. Instead of disruption, what unfolded was a testament to the efficacy of project-based learning. These students, selected at random apart from excluding "gifted" or "highly qualified" students, engaged in their self-chosen projects within multi-age groups. The environment was alive with quiet collaboration as they pursued their interests. One student even took charge of attendance by passing around a clipboard, a role performed seamlessly. Inquisitively, the evaluators inquired about the harmony they witnessed.

On that particular day:

One group deconstructed a donated motor, driven by their curiosity to comprehend its inner workings. What started as an exploration culminated in a comprehensive presentation analyzing various motor fuels and their global climate impacts, aligning with our earth science curriculum.

At a nearby table, another group crafted clay models of planets, complemented by a video illustrating the scale of planets when compared to our school acting as the sun scaled down to seventeen inches in diameter. This creative endeavor addressed multiple science and math objectives. Furthermore, they collaborated with our English teacher to delve into the evolution of optics and telescopes.

Meanwhile, a separate group engaged in crafting flower paper and ink for a calligraphy project, using plants cultivated in our school garden. The introduction of an adult volunteer enriched their experience. When they attended a calligrapher's assembly who designed pencils using a metal lathe, their interest pivoted towards learning calligraphy. Although not initially aligned with our objectives, they ingeniously justified its integration into our earth science curriculum.

This pattern extended across all eight projects, creating a hands-on learning environment that creatively aligned with state standards. In our outdoor garden, a living testament to three years of projects flourished. This group project setup liberated my time, enabling me to provide individualized attention, ensure completed readings, grade assignments, expand vocabulary, and foster math's relevance to each project. This integrated approach reverberated throughout their other classes, amplifying my lesson's impact. Ultimately, the garden emerged as our central hub for holistic integration.

The data showed significantly improved scores in math and science over three years and many students, as they left us to attend high school, tested in to the "gifted" category for the first time. Our standardized test scores were some of the highest in the state leading to our team's award as Team of the Year and to invitations to present our research with our University of Ga partners nationally.

This episode underscores how project-based learning transformed my classroom into a dynamic hub of exploration, learning, and innovation. It highlights the power of nurturing student interests to achieve learning objectives while organically fostering collaboration and critical thinking.

Inquiry-based Learning in STEM

Inquiry-based learning is an approach to teaching and learning that focuses on asking questions and seeking answers. In STEM education, inquiry-based learning is an effective way to engage students in the scientific process and help them develop critical thinking skills.

Benefits of Inquiry-Based Learning in STEM

Inquiry-based learning has several benefits for STEM education. First, it encourages students to take an active role in their learning. Instead of simply memorizing facts and formulas, students are encouraged to explore and discover information on their own. This can lead to a deeper understanding of the subject matter and a greater sense of ownership over the learning process.

Second, inquiry-based learning can help students develop critical thinking skills. By asking questions, students learn to analyze information, evaluate evidence, and draw conclusions. These skills are essential in STEM fields, where problem-solving is a key component of the work.

There are levels of inquiry from a novice problem solver to expert. This chart gives an overview of the basis of inquiry in a classroom project. Inquiry-based learning can help students develop a love of learning. When students are engaged in the learning process and feel like they are discovering new information, they are more likely to be motivated to continue learning and pursuing STEM subjects.

Levels of Inquiry

Problem Type	Problem Solving Level	Problem	Methodology	Solution
Tame	Novice	Given	Given	Given
Tame	Beginner	Given	Given	Unknown
Tame-Complex	Intermediate	Given	Unknown	Unknown
Wicked Messy	Expert	Unknown	Unknown	Unknown

Implementing Inquiry-Based Learning in Your Classroom:

Implementing inquiry-based learning in your classroom can be challenging, but there are several strategies you can use to make it more effective. Here are some practical tips for implementing inquiry-based learning in your STEM classroom:

Start with a question: Begin each lesson with a question that students will explore throughout the lesson. This will help focus their attention and give them a sense of purpose.

Provide guidance: While inquiry-based learning is student-driven, it is important to provide guidance and support along the way. Provide resources and scaffolding to help students explore the question and develop their understanding.

Encourage collaboration: Inquiry-based learning works best when students work together to explore the question. Encourage collaboration and discussion among students to deepen their understanding.

Celebrate the process: In inquiry-based learning, the process is just as important as the final product. Celebrate the process of learning and discovery, even if the students do not arrive at a definitive answer.

Inquiry-based learning is an effective approach to teaching and learning in STEM education. By encouraging students to ask questions and seek answers, inquiry-based learning can help students develop critical thinking skills, a love of learning, and a deeper understanding of STEM subjects. By implementing practical strategies in your classroom, you can make inquiry- based learning a success for your students.

Reflections on 5 Es:

Using the 5 E's with one of your Favorite Lessons.
This is my version of this model. Yours may differ. Here is a succinct breakdown of the 5E Model's five phases:

1. ENGAGE: The initial step revolves around the teacher assessing students' current knowledge and pinpointing gaps. Here, learners get their first glimpse of the new concept. This stage also aims to pique students' curiosity about upcoming topics. The instructor might ask students to pose questions or jot down their understanding of the subject. I like to use those wow experiments. Placing a cup of water on a board with ropes attached to the board. Swing the board in a circle as kids watch the cup of water go upside down without spilling or splashing them with water. That is a wow moment. Then teach centrifugal force.

2. EXPLORE: At this juncture, students delve into the topic actively through hands-on experiences. They might engage in the scientific process, collaborating with classmates to make observations. This offers a tactile approach to learning. In professional development workshops, we use this time to experience several stations. Students can also go through six or so stations in groups of 3-4. Stations can allow students to play with static electricity, handle magnets, plant seeds, mix chemicals or create paper airplanes.

3. EXPLAIN: In this instructor-guided stage, students consolidate their new knowledge and seek any necessary clarifications. An effective approach involves students recounting their discoveries from the 'Explore' stage, after which the teacher introduces detailed insights. Multimedia tools like videos or software might also be employed to enhance comprehension.

4. ELABORATE: This phase centers on allowing students to apply their newly acquired knowledge, facilitating a richer understanding. Educators might prompt students to craft presentations or embark on further explorations, ensuring the knowledge takes root. This might offer a setting in which a student's interest can guide how they pursue this topic.

5. EVALUATE: Evaluation within the 5E Model spans both informal and formal assessments. The evaluation can also encompass self-evaluations, peer reviews, written tasks, and tests.

VI: Assessing STEM Learning
Embrace the Rubric

Assessing student learning is an essential part of any teacher's job, and that holds true for STEM education as well. STEM education is unique in that it incorporates multiple subjects and skills, making it challenging to assess students' understanding comprehensively. However, there are different ways to assess STEM learning that can help teachers gauge their students' progress effectively. It does not always look like pencil and paper tests. This one has several forms depending on the age of students with ranges of points for each of the four parts of the rubric.

Project-based assessments: STEM education relies heavily on hands-on learning, and project-based assessments are ideal for assessing student understanding in this context. Teachers can assign projects that require students to apply their knowledge to real-world problems, and evaluate their performance based on the quality of their solutions.

Published Rubrics can help set goals and streamline evaluation. Rubrics give a range of points for the parts of a project that will be judged.

Collaboration assessments: Collaboration is an essential part of STEM education, and teachers can assess how well students work together by assigning group projects. Teachers can evaluate students based on a Rubric that sets out goals with respect to their ability to collaborate effectively, communicate their ideas, and problem-solve together.

Formative assessments: Formative assessments are an ongoing evaluation of students' understanding, and they can be used to identify areas where students need more support. Teachers can use quizzes, exit tickets, and other informal assessments to gauge students' understanding of a particular topic.

Performance assessments: Performance assessments involve students demonstrating their understanding of a particular concept or skill. For example, a teacher might ask students to design and build a simple machine, then evaluate their performance based on how well they meet specific criteria. Again, those criteria should be clearly set forth in a rubric.

Self-assessments: Self-assessments are a useful tool for promoting metacognition and encouraging students to take ownership of their learning. Teachers can ask students to reflect on their progress, identify areas where they need improvement, and set goals for the future.

The International STEM League publishes project rubrics. Students upload their project log books and presentations, then use an app to self-assess and award themselves points according to their adherence to the rubric. Judges provide feedback and allow for changes to be made by students prior to awarding final points to the projects.

It is possible to use apps to let students self-evaluate with the knowledge that their evaluation points may change when the teacher grades projects using the same rubric and awards final points. Self-evaluation can identify how a student may need additional clarification.

These methods are examples of authentic ways to assess STEM learning that can help teachers evaluate their students' understanding effectively. Project-based assessments, collaboration assessments, formative assessments, performance assessments, and self-assessments are all valuable tools that can help teachers gauge their students' progress and identify areas where they need more support. By using a variety of assessment methods, STEM teachers can ensure that they are meeting the needs of all their students and promoting their success in the classroom.

iNSL TEAMS

iNSL 5 Tool Stadium Project & Presentation Rubric

Category/Points	1	2	3	4
Is the scale model project accurate?	The project has some aspects that are correctly modeled, but most are not.	About half of the model is accurate.	The model is mostly accurate, but a few dimensions are slightly off.	The project is correctly modeled and the scale is consistent throughout.
Does the scale model project look like you put in a lot of effort?	The project was extremely simple, but one or two elements of detail were added to make it more complex. Some effort was put in to make the project good.	The project was somewhat complex, but no elements of detail were added. Some effort was put in to the project to make it look good.	The project was somewhat complex and elements of detail were added. A good amount of effort was put in to the project to make it look good.	The project was more complex or many details were added to make the project more complex. It is clear that a lot of time and effort were spent on making the project look good.
Did you complete the presentation including drawings?	The presentation is mostly complete and one drawing is attached.	The presentation is complete with drawings and graphics attached.	The presentation and model are complete including scale drawings & logbook.	The project is full realized and presented to the "press" including scale model & drawings.
Are the stadium areas clearly marked & present?	Areas are clearly marked but without graphic design.	Signage is present for all areas but sloppy or hastily completed.	Signs and markings are present through the stadium with clear graphics.	The stadium is has clear signage, finished graphics, and logos throughout.
Were you an effective presenter?	"Um" and "like" were said a lot throughout. You were nervous and unsure of what to say. No visual aids were used for the presentation.	There is evidence of some practice. While you might be nervous, you knew what you wanted to say and used an appropriate volume. Visual aids were used.		You were confident and did not use the words "um" or "like" frequently. You used an appropriate volume and used visual aids.

5 Tool Baseball Stadium Design Project Model Project Activity—Rubrics INSL International STEM League ©Copyright 2021 All Rights Reserved

Using Technology to Assess STEM learning

Assessment is a vital component of any STEM education program. It is the process of gathering information about what students know and can do and using that information to make decisions about instruction and learning. Technology can play a significant role in facilitating assessment in STEM education.

One of the most popular ways of using technology to assess STEM learning is through online quizzes and assessments. These tools allow teachers to create and distribute quizzes and tests to students electronically.

Online quizzes and assessments are easy to administer and grade, and they provide instant feedback to students. Teachers can also use online quizzes and assessments to track student progress throughout the school year.

Virtual simulations and labs are another way in which technology can be used to assess STEM learning. These tools allow students to engage in hands-on activities and experiments in a virtual environment. Virtual simulations and labs are particularly useful in situations where access to physical equipment or materials is limited. Teachers can use virtual simulations and labs to assess students' understanding of scientific concepts and their ability to apply that understanding in a practical context.

Data analytics and visualization tools can help teachers to assess STEM learning by analyzing student performance data. These tools can provide insights into student strengths and weaknesses, as well as patterns of learning across the class. With data analytics and visualization tools, teachers can identify areas where students need additional support, and adjust their instruction accordingly.

Technology can be a valuable tool in assessing STEM learning. Online quizzes and assessments, virtual simulations and labs, and data analytics and visualization tools are just a few examples of how technology can be used to support assessment in STEM education. By leveraging the power of technology, teachers can gain deeper insights into student learning and provide more targeted instruction and support.

Strategies for Providing Feedback on STEM Projects
As a STEM teacher, providing feedback on student projects is an essential aspect of your job. Feedback is not assessment but a step in the engineering design process.

Feedback helps students understand their strengths and weaknesses, identifies areas of improvement, and encourages them to strive for excellence. However, delivering feedback can be a daunting task, especially if you are a new teacher.

To help you provide constructive feedback, here are some effective strategies that you can use in your classroom.

- **Start with positive feedback:** Begin by highlighting the strengths of the project. This approach helps students feel appreciated and motivates them to work harder. It also sets a positive tone for the rest of the feedback.
- **Be specific:** Vague feedback can be confusing for students. Be specific about what you like and what needs improvement. For example, instead of saying "good job," you can say "I liked your clear explanation of scientific concepts."
- **Provide Rubrics:** If rubrics were provided for presentations, logbooks, project plan, and lab reports, giving feedback is more targeted and effective.
- **Use the sandwich technique:** This technique involves starting and ending with positive feedback and placing constructive criticism in the middle. This approach helps students feel motivated to improve.
- **Avoid criticism:** Avoid using negative language that demotivates students. Instead, provide specific suggestions for improvement.
- **Focus on the process, not just the product:** It is essential to focus on the process of creating the project, not just the final product. Encourage the growth mindset. This approach helps students understand the importance of planning, research, and problem-solving skills.
- **Encourage self-reflection:** Encouraging students to reflect on their work and identify areas of improvement helps them take ownership

of their learning. It helps them become more self-aware and confident.

- **Provide opportunities for revision:** Giving students the opportunity to revise their work based on feedback helps them learn from their mistakes and improve their skills.

Data tells the story that matters. Assess before, during, and after a lesson or activity to be sure that students are learning what you are teaching. Adjust how and what you teach based on those assessments. Providing feedback on STEM projects is an integral part of teaching. By using these strategies, you can help your students understand their strengths and weaknesses, motivate them to improve, and encourage them to continue learning. Remember to focus on the process, be specific and constructive, and encourage self-reflection. By doing so, you will help your students become confident and successful STEM learners.

VII: Changing the sysSTEM
Addressing Common Misconceptions about STEM

STEM education has gained a lot of popularity in recent years because of its potential to equip students with the skills and knowledge required to thrive in the 21st-century workplace. However, despite its numerous benefits, there are still some misconceptions associated with STEM education. In this section, we will address some of these misconceptions and help teachers understand the true essence of STEM education.

Misconception 1: STEM education is only for high-achieving students.

One of the most common misconceptions associated with STEM education is that it is only suitable for high-achieving students. However, this is not true. STEM education is for all students, regardless of their academic abilities.

The goal of STEM education is to equip students with the skills and knowledge required to succeed in the 21st-century workplace. Therefore, it is essential to provide all students with access to STEM education and support them in developing the necessary skills.

Misconception 2: STEM education is only for students who want to pursue STEM careers.

Another misconception associated with STEM education is that it is only for students who want to pursue STEM careers. However, this is also not true. STEM education provides students with a diverse range of skills and knowledge that can be applied to various fields. For example, the critical thinking, problem-solving, and analytical skills developed through STEM education can be applied to fields such as finance, law, and healthcare.

Misconception 3: STEM education is only about memorizing facts and figures.

Another common misconception associated with STEM education is that it is only about memorizing facts and figures. However, this is not true. STEM education is about developing critical thinking, problem-solving, and analytical skills. These skills are developed through hands-on activities and projects that require students to apply their knowledge to real-world problems.

Misconception 4: STEM education is only for students who are good at math.

Another misconception associated with STEM education is that it is only for students who are good at math. However, this is certainly not true. STEM education requires students to have a diverse range of skills, including critical thinking, problem-solving, and analytical skills. While math is an essential component of STEM education, students who struggle with math can still excel in STEM education and technology offers help in this area.

STEM education is an essential component of modern education, and it is essential to address the misconceptions associated with it. By understanding the true essence of STEM education, teachers can provide all students with access to STEM education and support them in developing the necessary skills to succeed in the 21st-century workplace.

Dealing with Student Disengagement in STEM

Dealing with student disengagement in STEM is a common challenge that many teachers face. As a STEM educator, it is important to recognize that disengagement can be caused by various factors such as lack of interest, difficulty in understanding, and boredom.

However, there are several strategies that teachers can implement to re-engage students and promote a love for STEM. Post-COVID, the issue of engaging students has become a top priority. Too many students who had to learn at home in less than ideal settings have come to think of school as optional. One of the most effective ways to combat disengagement is to make STEM education relevant and relatable to students' lives. Teachers can do this by incorporating real-world examples and applications into their lessons.

For instance, if teaching math, teachers can relate equations to everyday scenarios such as calculating the distance a car travels or the cost of groceries. This helps students understand the importance of STEM in their daily lives and makes the subject more interesting.

Another strategy is to incorporate hands-on activities and projects that allow students to apply what they learn in real-life scenarios. This helps students see the practical application of STEM and promotes a deeper understanding of the subject. Teachers can also encourage collaboration among students by assigning group projects that require teamwork and communication skills.

It is also important to create a positive and supportive classroom environment. Teachers can do this by praising students' efforts and acknowledging their achievements. This helps build confidence and encourages students to take risks and ask questions. Teachers can also provide personalized feedback and support to students who are struggling, which can help them feel more engaged and motivated.

In addition, technology can be used to enhance STEM education and promote engagement. Teachers can incorporate interactive software and apps that allow students to explore STEM concepts in a fun and engaging way. This not only makes learning more enjoyable but also helps students retain information better.

In conclusion, dealing with student disengagement in STEM requires patience, creativity, and a willingness to adapt teaching strategies. By making STEM education relevant, hands-on, collaborative, and fun, teachers can help students see the value of STEM and promote a lifelong love for learning.

Supporting Struggling Learners in STEM

Supporting struggling learners in STEM can be a challenging task for any teacher.

However, with the right strategies and practical tips, you can help struggling learners to overcome their difficulties and achieve success in STEM subjects.

One of the first steps to supporting struggling learners in STEM is to identify the areas where they are struggling. This can be done through observation, assessment, and feedback from the students themselves. Once you identify the areas where the student is struggling, you can develop a plan to address those specific areas.

Having students collect data in a middle grades classroom and calculate a score from their data allowed a teacher to identify the one fundamental error in how a student treated mixed fractions. Once remediated, the student was offered additional ways to practice place value and estimation so that they could better identify an answer that was not reasonable.

In another classroom a high school engineering teacher who took part in a special event argued that her "highly capable" students should be allowed to use calculators to calculate their scores, but relented when the presenter insisted on paper and pencil for at least the first round of data collection. At the end of the lesson, the teacher and her colleagues had to regroup as they learned that students who were the top of their classes and planning to attend college in one year were unable to accurately read minutes and parts of a second on an analog stop watch, struggled to measure out a track length longer than the tape measure they were using and could not correctly average the times of all the timers for a run of the radio controlled car.

Over reliance on tools that do the work for you before you learn to do it for yourself is leaving huge gaps in what students learn. Hand-on activities offer one solution.

Mentors offer another effective support for struggling learners in STEM. Providing one-on-one support or tutoring sessions gives student the extra attention they may need. College chapters of national organizations such as the ASA (American Statistics Association) and NSBE (National Society of Black Engineers) are examples of kids willing to help as near peer mentors. The adults in these organizations often hold Saturday meetings with groups of students and foster STEM through academic competitions like the International STEM League or Vex Robotics. Daily exercises that build a sense of comfort with basic scale, computation, and measurement can help students grow in their comfort with mathematics.

Scaleville is a series of these daily activities that a teacher can use as bell ringers to grow a sense of number and estimation. After using such interventions, students can recognize an unreasonable answer because they have developed a sense of how much things weigh, how fast they move, how much area they cover and what powers of ten can do to help in estimation. These also help teachers build that same sense of scale. It was ignored in most teacher education paths. Therefore, it gets ignored when we teach. This is an example of a Scaleville daily activity that can be used over one day or a week. There are activity books for elementary, middle, and high school classes.

Distance and Speed
Activity 53

Step # 1

Remember our 14 to 18 feet-tall giraffe? What is its top running speed?

Why would a giraffe need to run?
Who would chase a giraffe?

Step # 2

Name something 10 times as fast.

Name something $1/10^{th}$ as fast.

Step # 3

Convert the measurement from # 1 to metric, or convert to standard if already in metric.

Step # 4

The measurement from #1 falls between what two powers of ten?

☐   ☐
10   and   10

scaleville

53

Another strategy that can be used to support struggling learners in STEM is to adjust your teaching methods to better suit their learning style. For example, if a student is struggling with a concept that is presented verbally, you may want to provide visual aids or hands-on activities to help them better understand the material.

It can also be helpful to break down complex concepts into smaller, more manageable pieces. This can help struggling learners to better understand the material and build confidence as they see their progress. I usually lean into the data, but this is one instance in which I am not convinced that the studies can isolate the variables well enough to tell me this does not work, so I would try it because it seems like a reasonable strategy

.

Finally, it is important to encourage struggling learners in STEM to persevere and not give up. Reassure them that it is okay to make mistakes and that learning is a process. Provide positive feedback and celebrate their successes, no matter how small. Always remember the STEM Mindset includes the Growth Mindset. Supporting struggling learners in STEM can be a challenging task, but with the right strategies and support, you can help these students to achieve success and build confidence in their abilities.

Addressing the Gender Gap in STEM

STEM (Science, Technology, Engineering, and Mathematics) fields have traditionally been male dominated. The gender gap in STEM is a significant concern that needs to be addressed. According to the National Science Foundation, women earn only 20% of bachelor's degrees in engineering, 18% in computer science, and 43% in mathematics. This gap is not only unjust; it also limits the potential talent pool for these critical fields.

Teachers play a crucial role in closing the gender gap in STEM. Here are some practical tips and strategies that can help teachers address this issue:

Foster a welcoming and inclusive classroom environment: Teachers can create a welcoming classroom environment that is inclusive of all genders. They can encourage students to share their experiences and ideas without fear of judgment or ridicule. Teachers can also use examples and case studies that feature women in STEM to inspire and encourage female students.

Create a Who's-Who file box (virtual or real) organized by topics you teach in your main subject area and in STEM fields. Behind each one, place examples of people who we should know about, but may not. Do not be exclusive but inclusive. This makes it simple to give examples that include various genders and ethnicities and races when that teachable moment arrives.

Provide mentorship and role models: Female students in STEM often lack role models and mentors who can guide and inspire them. Teachers can help by connecting their female students with successful women in STEM fields and in their own communities. They can also serve as role models themselves by sharing their experiences and successes in STEM fields.

Use gender-neutral language: Teachers should avoid gender-specific language when teaching STEM in their lectures, assignments, and tests. This will help create a more inclusive learning environment and make female students feel more comfortable and welcome. It is enlightening when we learn how often we say "he."

Encourage collaboration: Teachers can encourage collaboration among their students, especially between male and female students. Collaborative projects and group work can help break down gender barriers and promote teamwork and inclusivity. Make sure that on hands on projects, male roles do not always have the males doing the "fun" part while the females calculate and write the lab reports.

Celebrate diversity: Finally, teachers should celebrate diversity in their classrooms. They can organize events and activities that celebrate the accomplishments of women and minorities in STEM fields.

Closing the gender gap in STEM is a critical goal that requires the support and commitment of all educators. By creating a welcoming and inclusive classroom environment, providing mentorship and role models, using gender-neutral language, encouraging collaboration, and celebrating diversity, teachers can help address this issue and inspire the next generation of female STEM professionals.

VIII: Professional Development and Resources

Yes, workshops can really feel as exciting as this one.

These teachers were new to the field and excited to be integrating science, computer science, and mathematics with an engineering program. In a one-week STEM Sprint, they experienced it as a student and learned to facilitate it as a teacher. They used an Esports game as the HOOK for their kids and their classrooms were exciting places this year.

STEM education is a rapidly evolving field. As a teacher, it is essential to stay updated on the latest developments and best practices in STEM education to ensure that your students receive the best education possible. Fortunately, there are many opportunities for professional development in STEM education that can help you improve your teaching skills and stay up to date with the latest trends.

Attend Conferences and Workshops

Conferences and workshops are an excellent way to learn from experts in the field and connect with other STEM educators. Many conferences and workshops offer hands-on learning opportunities, keynote speakers, and networking events that can help you stay current with the latest trends and best practices in STEM education.

Some popular conferences and workshops for STEM educators include the National Science Teachers Association (NSTA) Conference, the International Society for Technology in Education (ISTE) Conference, and the STEM Conference for Educators. You may find that your budget and needs are better served by attending more local and state level conferences.

Join Professional Organizations

Professional organizations like the National Science Teachers Association (NSTA), the National Council of Teachers of Mathematics (NCTM), and the National Association of Biology Teachers (NABT) offer a wealth of resources and opportunities for STEM educators. These organizations provide access to professional development resources, networking opportunities, and the latest research and best practices in STEM education.

Take Online Courses and Webinars

Online courses and webinars are convenient options for STEM educators who want to continue their professional development without leaving their homes. Many online platforms, such as Coursera, Udemy, and edX, offer free or low-cost courses on a variety of STEM topics. Khan Academy can help you fill in your own gaps should that increase your confidence. It is a great refresher for math concepts.

Participate in Mentoring Programs

Mentoring programs are another excellent way for STEM educators to develop their skills and knowledge. Many schools and professional organizations offer mentoring programs that pair experienced teachers with novice educators.

Mentoring programs provide opportunities for new teachers to learn from experienced educators, receive feedback on their teaching, and gain valuable insights into the teaching profession.

Professional development is essential for STEM educators who want to stay current with the latest trends and best practices in the field. Attending conferences and workshops, joining professional organizations, taking online courses and webinars, and participating in mentoring programs are just a few of the many opportunities available for STEM educators to continue their professional growth and development. By taking advantage of these opportunities, you can improve your teaching skills, enhance your students' learning experience, and advance your career as a STEM educator.

STEM Resources for Teachers

STEM education is rapidly growing and is becoming an essential part of every student's academic journey. However, teaching STEM subjects can be challenging, especially for new teachers. And to help them with their teaching journey, here are some STEM resources for teachers that can aid them in delivering quality education and help students develop their STEM skills.

International STEM League- the iNSL is a 501c3 organization that provides a practice league for STEM careers. It has curriculum for K-12 project based learning and has recently created an Academic Esports Curriculum to use in conjunction with Gaming. iNSL runs an international STEM competition with an annual points race.
http://www.insl.org
Sprint workshops are available through the International STEM League now. https://www.insl.org/design-sprints

National Science Teaching Association - The National Science Teaching Association is a professional organization that supports science teachers in the United States. They provide resources such as lesson plans, professional development opportunities, and instructional materials for teachers.

Code.org - Code.org offers free, online coding courses for students of all ages. The website also provides teacher training and resources for teaching computer science.

NASA Education - NASA Education provides educators with resources, materials, and opportunities for professional development in STEM education. The website offers lesson plans and multimedia resources teachers to bring into classrooms.

PBS Learning Media - PBS Learning Media is an online library of K-12 educational resources, including STEM education materials. The website offers lesson plans, videos, and interactive activities that promote inquiry- based learning.

Art of STEM – Art of STEM brings blended learning to new heights with on site Art of STEM Festivals for elementary students and families. It has a suite of programs, classes, camps, and kits for remote and in person learning.

Ten80 Education – In its 17th year of national and international competition, this group offers effective STEM classes, camps, and curriculum as well as competitions

Teaching STEM subjects can be challenging, but with the right resources, teachers can deliver quality education and help students develop their STEM skills. These STEM resources for teachers can provide support, inspiration, and guidance to educators who are committed to promoting STEM education.

Building a STEM Teacher Network

As a STEM teacher, it is essential to build a network of like-minded educators who share a passion for science, technology, engineering, and math. Collaborating with other teachers can help you improve your teaching skills, stay current with the latest trends in STEM education, and create a supportive community of professionals.

Here are some tips for building a STEM teacher network:

Join Professional Organizations: Joining a professional organization is an excellent way to connect with other STEM teachers. You can attend conferences, workshops, and webinars, which provide opportunities to learn from experts in the field, network with other educators, and share your own experiences.

Connect on Social Media: Social media platforms like Twitter, LinkedIn, and Facebook are great places to connect with other STEM teachers. You can join groups and participate in discussions, share resources, and ask for help and advice.

Attend Local STEM Events: Attending local STEM events like science fairs, hackathons, and maker fairs can help you connect with other STEM teachers in your area. These events provide opportunities to learn about new teaching strategies, share ideas, and collaborate on projects.

Join Online Communities: Online communities like STEM Teaching Tools, Edmodo, and STEM Learning Communities offer a wealth of resources and support for STEM teachers. These communities provide a platform to ask questions, share teaching strategies, and collaborate with other educators.

Collaborate on Projects: Collaborating on STEM projects with other teachers can help you develop new teaching strategies, share resources, and create a supportive community of professionals. You can work together on projects like robotics competitions, coding challenges, and science experiments.

Building a network of STEM teachers is essential for professional development, staying current with the latest trends in STEM education, and creating a supportive community of professionals. Joining professional organizations, connecting on social media, attending local STEM events, joining online communities, and collaborating on projects are all great ways to build your network.

IX: Inspiring the Next Generation of Data Driven Global Problem Solvers

What characterizes a confident teacher?

- A confident teacher does not have all the answers, and is comfortable admitting that is the case.
- The confident teacher knows how to access resources to find answers or point students in the right direction for exploration
- The confident teacher knows how to experiment if that presents a better next step toward understanding.
- The confident teacher is an enthusiastic life-long learner who updates basic STEM skills to better serve students.

That is why professional development is so important. Having clarified this definition of teaching with confidence, why is it so important?

The students you teach are looking for guidance and knowledge from you. They need you to be confident in your abilities to teach them the skills and concepts that will help them succeed in their future careers. Additionally, a confident teacher can inspire confidence in their students, which can lead to greater engagement and better learning outcomes.

To teach with confidence, it is important to stay up to date with the latest research and developments in your field, as well as seeking out professional development opportunities to improve your own teaching skills.

When you have a deep understanding of the subject matter, you can answer questions and provide explanations with ease and can find reliable sources when you need to know more.

Your comfort with the subject matter and with the things you do not know will help build your students' confidence in the subject matter as well. You will also better identify the subject matter intersections between your primary subject and others.

Another way to teach with confidence is to be prepared. This means having lesson plans and materials ready in advance, and anticipating potential challenges or questions that may arise during your lesson. Being prepared also allows you to be flexible when those teachable moments happen.

Prepared does not mean adhering to the lesson plan when better teaching opportunities arise. By being well-prepared, you can focus more on teaching and engaging with your students, rather than worrying about logistics.

Additionally, it is important to foster a positive classroom culture that encourages experimentation and learning from mistakes. This can help students feel more comfortable taking risks and asking questions, which can lead to greater engagement and understanding of the subject matter.

Always remember that teaching with confidence is not about being perfect or knowing everything. It is about being comfortable with the subject matter and being willing to learn alongside your students. By modeling a growth mindset and a willingness to learn, you can inspire your students to do the same and create a classroom culture that values curiosity and rewards exploration.

X: Cultivate a Passion for STEM!

Being passionate about STEM as a teacher is a powerful force that ignites curiosity, sparks inspiration, and propels students on a lifelong journey of discovery. It is a genuine dedication to fostering a love for science, technology, engineering, and mathematics that goes beyond the classroom walls.

Passion for STEM is evident in a teacher's unwavering commitment to creating engaging learning experiences. It means designing hands-on experiments that captivate students' imaginations, encouraging them to ask questions, make connections, and explore the world around them. It is about infusing real-world context into lessons, enabling students to see the relevance and applicability of STEM in their everyday lives.

Passion for STEM shines through in a teacher's contagious enthusiasm and genuine excitement for the subject matter. It means staying current with the latest advancements, embracing new technologies and teaching methodologies, and constantly seeking out opportunities for professional growth.

A passionate STEM teacher not only imparts knowledge but also inspires a lifelong love for learning and an insatiable curiosity that extends far beyond the classroom. Ultimately, being passionate about STEM as a teacher means being a catalyst for change, nurturing the next generation of innovators, problem-solvers, and critical thinkers who will shape our future.

A passionate STEM teacher is a relentless advocate for equity and inclusion, ensuring that all students, regardless of their background or gender, feel welcomed and empowered in the pursuit of their interests. They strive to break down barriers, challenge stereotypes, and foster a diverse and inclusive learning environment where everyone has the opportunity to thrive and succeed. It means instilling in students the belief that they have the power to make a difference and contribute to the world through their STEM knowledge and skills.

Passion for STEM is a transformative force that fuels the fire of learning, unlocks potential, and empowers students to reach new heights. It is this passion that lights the way, guiding students on a path of endless possibilities and inspiring them to embrace the wonders of STEM with open hearts and curious minds.

Sample Lessons

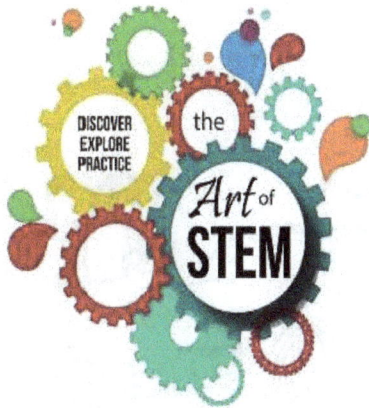

POM POM CATAPULTS

Materials:
5 craft sticks, 2 tongue depressors, 4 rubber bands, bottle cap, pom-poms, cardstock for bullseye, ruler, pencil, tape

Description: Investigate lever and fulcrum (simple machines) with fuzzy pom poms and a pop stick catapult. The catapult is basically a lever. A lever is a simple machine with a beam on a fixed hinge, or fulcrum. A lever is rigid but can see-saw on its fulcrum. The catapult stores energy when its arm is pulled down over the fulcrum. Energy is released to launch the pom pom payload.
Where should you place the fulcrum to store the most energy and create the longest launch?

USE DATA TO FIND THE BEST PLACE FOR YOUR CATAPULT'S FULCRUM

START HERE

A catapult uses the sudden release of stored potential energy to launch its payload. Types of catapults have been used by the Greeks, Romans, and Chinese. Early catapults tried to increase the range and power of a crossbow. A Greek historian was the first to document a mechanical arrow firing catapult (called a Ballista) in 399 BC. Our catapult is a small scale machine that will launch fuzzy pom poms.

CONSTRUCT AND INVESTIGATE

1. Turn one of the tongue depressors into a ruler by marking centimeters or inches along the stick. This allows you to collect data on the best place to put your crossbar given the target's distance and height.
2. Stack and band together 5 pop sticks.
3. Band the tongue depressors at tip and criss-crossed over the crossbar.
4. Glue or tape the cap (experiment with attaching the cap as a variable).

COLLECT AND ANALYZE DATA

Put the projectile into the cap, hold down the top stick, release and watch the object fly. Practice aiming by setting up a target.
These numbers will help you decide the best launch setup for your catapult.

Create a chart to collect the distance travelled vs. fulcrum placement.
- Write the fulcrum measurement on the chart (Independent Variable).
- Measure the distance travelled by each pom pom (Dependent Variable).

X Fulcrum Where is the beam?	Y Landing How far did the pom pom travel?
2 cm	300 centimeters

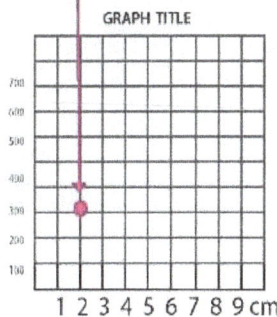

GRAPHS HELP DATA TELL STORIES

Move the chart data to a graph so the patterns in data are easy to read. The X axis along the base is an independent variable that you control. You control the location of your fulcrum. Y axis is the dependent variable that changes as a result of your decisions like the distance a pom pom travels. Place a finger on the X axis number. Place a finger on the matching Y axis number. Bring your fingers together and place a dot.

REDESIGN

What other "variables" can you test to change the catapult's launch power? Examples: Test rubber bands. Test number of pop sticks in your fulcrum. Collect data. Read the data, and redesign your catapult using data!

Driving STEM

FORCES & MOTION

Energy Bounce

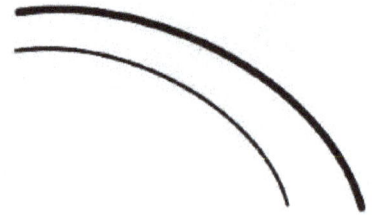

MATERIALS
4 different types of balls rubber
bands
tape measure handout
pencil

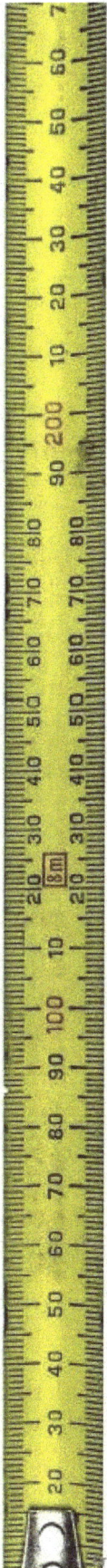

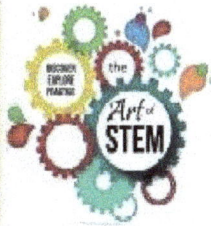

Forces & Motion
Energy Bounce

Energy Bounce
Procedures

Step 1
- Set the meter stick up vertically
- Hold the ball at the top of the meter stick and drop the ball. What force is acting on the ball?

- Does it bounce back the same distance it was dropped?

Step 2
- Measure and record how high the ball bounces when dropped from 4 ft...
- Drop 1 ___ Drop 2 ___ Drop 3 _____
- Is the height of the first bounce the same each time?
- What is the average bounce of the ball?.

Step 3
Drop the ball from various heights, 1 foot, 2 feet, 3 feet
- Graph the highest recoil of the ball from each height.

Step 4
Repeat steps 3 and 4 for each different kind of ball and add to the group data chart and graph.

5

87

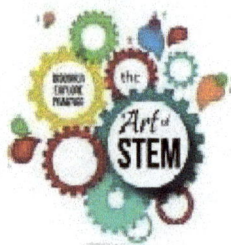

Forces & Motion
Energy Bounce

Energy Bounce

Energy cannot be created or destroyed but it can be changed in form.

Use 3 kinds of balls to determine if there is a pattern to the way balls bounce.

Essential Questions

- What is an elastic collision?
- What is stored energy?
- What is potential energy?
- What is kinetic energy?

Materials
- Golf Ball
- Ping Pong Ball
- Wiffle Ball
- Graph
- Colored pencils

7

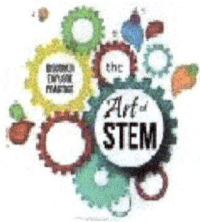

Forces & Motion
Energy Bounce

ENERGY BOUNCE DISCUSSION

Kinetic Energy describes the amount of energy an object has by virtue of it having some non-zero mass and traveling at some speed.
KE= 1/2 mv^2

Potential Energy describes the energy that could be gained by that object if it was not at that poten-tial. It is not really accurate to say that potential energy is energy at rest since it is very possible for moving objects to have potential energy.

A book sitting on a shelf has some gravitational energy. It's potential energy equals the amount of energy needed to put the book up there in the first place and the amount of energy which could be gained if the book falls down from the shelf. As the book is falling, before it hits the floor, the book has some fraction of its potential energy converted into kinetic, in other words it has both kinds of energy at the same time.

ENDURING UNDERSTANDING

1. Potential energy is energy that is stored in an object. If you stretch a rubber band, you will give it potential energy. As the rubber band is released, potential energy is changed to motion

2. Kinetic energy is energy of motion. A rubber band flying through the air has kinetic energy.

ESSENTIAL QUESTIONS

1.   What is the difference in kinetic and potential energy?
2.   What are some examples of energy transversions?

Look for Misconceptions
  Many students incorrectly assume that an object cannot have kinetic energy and potential energy at the same time.
  TRUTH: As objects convert PE to KE we can think of them as having both kinds of energy at the same time.

Forces & Motion
Energy Bounce

DIRECTIONS

Step 1: Set the meter stick up vertically, or hang a tape measure on the wall.
Hold the ball at the top of the meter stick and drop the ball.

What force is acting on the ball?

Does it bounce back the same distance it was dropped?

Step 2 : Measure and record how high the ball bounces when dropped from 4 ft.

Drop 1 ____ Drop 2 _____ Drop 3 _____ Average:_____

Is the height of the first bounce the same each time?
What is the average first recoil bounce of the ball?.

Step 3: Drop the ball from various heights, 1 foot, 2 feet, 3 feet
Graph the first or highest recoil of the ball from each height.

Step 4: Repeat steps 3 and 4 for each different kind of ball.
Add data to the chart and graph

Initial Drop Height	4 feet	5 feet	6 feet	8 feet	Dig Deeper: What is the ratio of recoil to drop height?
Ball 1 recoil height					
Ball 2 recoil height					
Ball 3 recoil height					
Ball 4 recoil height					

Average recoil heights _____   _____   _____   _____

Real Reverse Engineering

Art of STEM for Ten80 Education

Lesson Plan & Notes

Objectives

Critically examine something mechanical that you see in everyday life, but may not think much about, then ask and answer the question, "How does it work?". Explain how it works so that others can understand how it works simply by watching your video, reading your description and/or looking at your illustrations.

Science and Engineering Correlations

HS.PS-FE.c. Evaluate natural and designed systems where there is an exchange of energy between objects and fields and characterize how the energy is exchanged.

HS-ETS-ED.b. Analyze input and output data and functioning of a human-built system to define opportunities to improve the system's performance so it better meets the needs of end users while taking into account constraints.

HS.PS-E.h. Design, build, and evaluate devices that convert one form of energy into another form of energy.

MS.ETS-ED.f. Communicate information about a proposed solution to a problem, including relevant scientific principles, how the design was developed, how it meets the criteria and constraints of the problem, and how it reduces the potential for negative consequences for society and the natural environment.

HS-ETS-ED.b. Analyze input and output data and functioning of a human-built system performance so it better meets the needs of end users while taking into account constraints (e.g., materials, costs, scientific principles).

ELA Correlations

RST.6-10.7. Integrate quantitative or technical information expressed in words in a text with a version of that information expressed visually.

SL.6-12.1. Engage effectively in a range of collaborative discussions (one-on-one, in groups, and teacher led) with diverse partners on grade appropriate topics, texts, and issues, building on others' ideas and expressing their own clearly.

GATHER MATERIALS

- Wind-up toy or pull-back vehicle
- Phillips Screwdriver (small)
- Needle-Nose Pliers (optional)
- Measuring tape or ruler
- Logbook
- ClearTape
- *Tray to hold small parts*
- *Digital camera for documentation.*
    - *Take pictures as you go.*
    - *This is not part of the formal activity, but having images of each step helps with recall.*

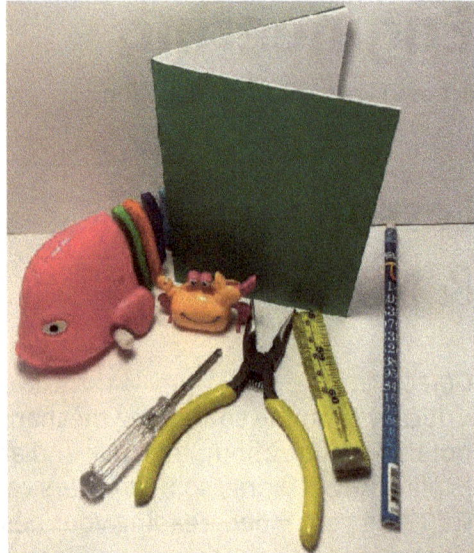

PREPARE WORKSPACES

PURPOSE

The purpose of this activity:

- **Multiple representations** – Provide opportunities to explore and discuss gears, GIP, energy and engineering in a different context

- **Practice GIP** – focus on observations and DOCUMENTATION. Your goal is to understand how it works and be able to communicate that to others through your writing and figures (not just verbally).

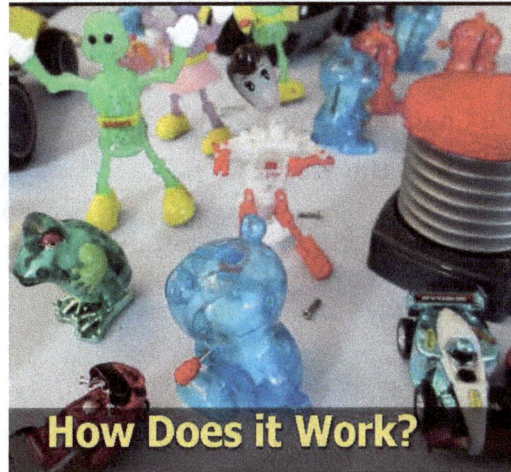

How Does it Work?

- **Reinforce lessons in energy** – your goal is to follow the energy from your hand through the mechanisms and movement. (Transformation of energy, kinetic, potential, etc.)

- **Foster Creativity** that often starts with sketches. Turn thoughts into tangible materials you can communicate to others.

Additional discussion on this idea.

Dream, Draw, Design

Dreams are often fueled by ideas, descriptions and pictures of places and things others have created, so without a base of knowledge and images to build upon, it is impossible for most of us to "dream up" things we don't already know about.

To convey your ideas to others, illustrations and sketches, are compelling tools. They are usually the first concrete step in making an idea you've created into a reality. Drawing and illustrating is a kind of language.

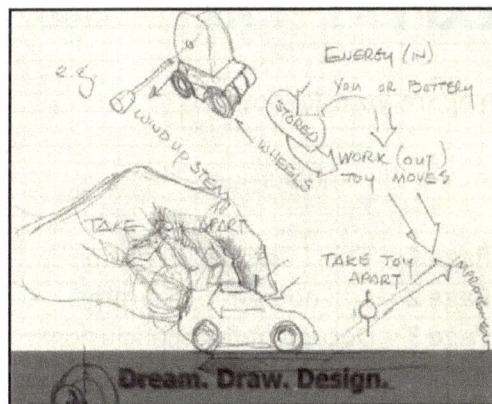

Dream. Draw. Design.

Design is the next step to transforming your dreams into something real. Taking a well defined idea and figuring out how to make it work is often a matter of choosing materials and defining manufacturing and testing processes through the application of scientific, mathematical and engineering analysis...but let's not go there yet.

Your first step to dreaming, drawing and designing truly new things, is building a mental library about how existing things work. Let's start building.

ENGAGE

The Challenge:

How Does this Work?

Wind, pull back, and demonstrate multiple toys to engage the audience. Issue the day's engineering "challenge."

"Your challenge is to reverse engineer something mechanical. Take apart a wind-up or 'rev' toy with the goal of understanding how it works and creatively (but accurately) communicating your new knowledge to others.

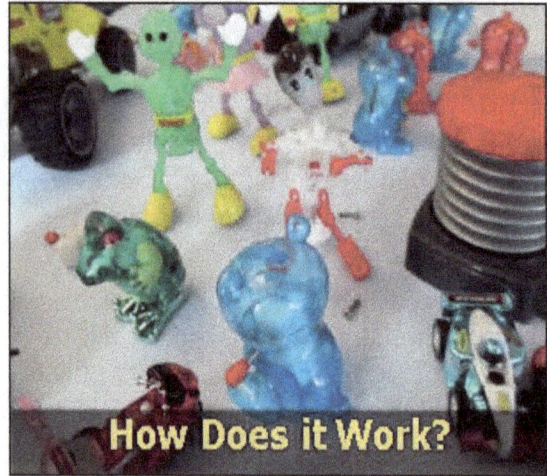

How Does it Work?

Your description should include the path of energy from your hand to ultimate movements of the toy. The path of energy will be stored and transformed in many ways. Use observations, reverse engineering, and detective work to explain that path."

EXPLAIN: Follow Good Documentation Practices = GIP

Prepare your logbook.

Enter a title and purpose.

Page 1 = Title, Purpose, Prediction
Page 2 = Add notes and diagrams.
Page 3 = Document final conclusions.
Illustrate the energy transfer from windup to full stop.

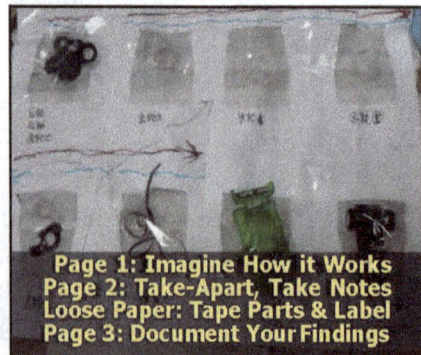

Page 1: Imagine How it Works
Page 2: Take-Apart, Take Notes
Loose Paper: Tape Parts & Label
Page 3: Document Your Findings

EXPLAIN: Injection Molded Toys

Before you start, look at a few common parts you'll find in the investigation.

This toy shown on the slide has the two main parts easily come apart with the removal of one screw on this toy. The blue body parts are simply 3 injection molded parts; front torso, back torso and legs.

Injection molding uses a hollow shaped mold and hot plastic (or other materials).

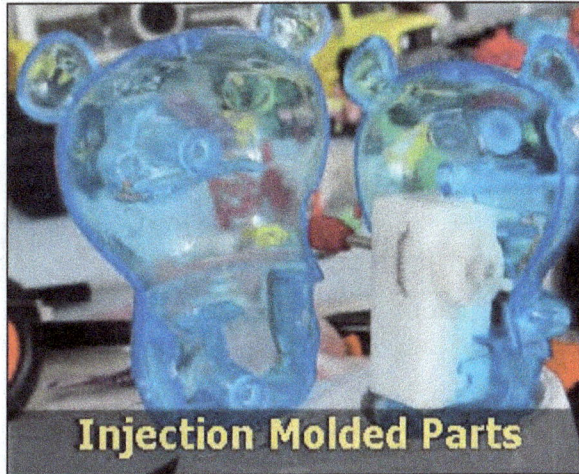

Injection Molded Parts

Read about injection molding with plastics <u>HERE</u>. https://www.thoughtco.com/what-is-injection-molding-820350
Learn about polymers used in injection molding <u>HERE</u>. https://www.thoughtco.com/definition-of-polymer-605912

What did you learn about injection molding and polymers?

EXPLORE – Preview the Project

Identify Parts

Draw what you see.

Tape parts to your notebook or paper

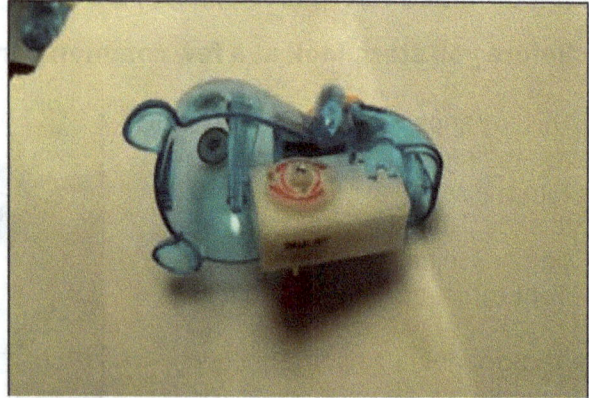

1. The Motor

The 'box' inside the toy is essentially its motor. Two pins can be seen opposite each other on the gear (colored red) on the outside of the motor.

When the motor turns, those pins turn and catch on the lever attached to the feet.

The little machine tilts enough to change its center of gravity. The wind up falls over.

Look for a motor box.

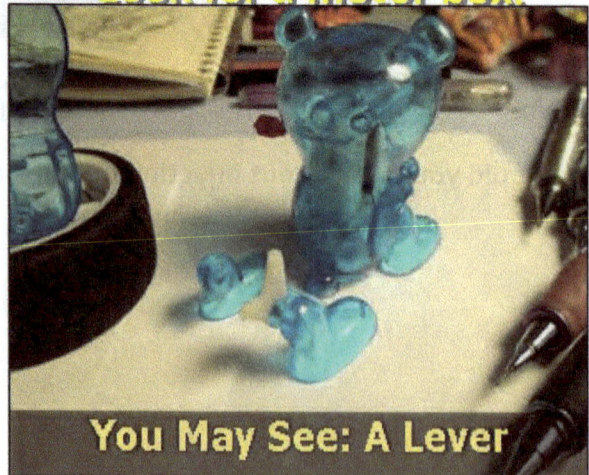

2. The Lever

What is a lever? This simple machine has a bar that moves on a fixed support, or fulcrum. Apply force by pushing **down** on one end of the lever to result in a force pushing **up** at the other end of the lever. Levers, like gears, can be used to increase the force available from a mechanical power source.

What does your lever do?

You May See: A Lever

3. Springs

When the machine tilts over, the spring stretches. When the spring clears the legs lever, the spring snaps back and makes the toy stand upright.

This spring action doesn't just make it stand upright. It makes the toy flip over backwards.

Draw your lever.

You May See: Springs

3b. Coiled spring in the Motor Box

Where does the energy to flip get stored when you wind up the toy?

There seems to be a split down the middle of the motor casing but no obvious way to open it. It is either glued together or a "forced fit". Place the box on a flat surface. Slide a screwdriver between the lines to split the box. Turn the tool into a lever as you GENTLY rock the tool back and forth to separate the two halves of the box.

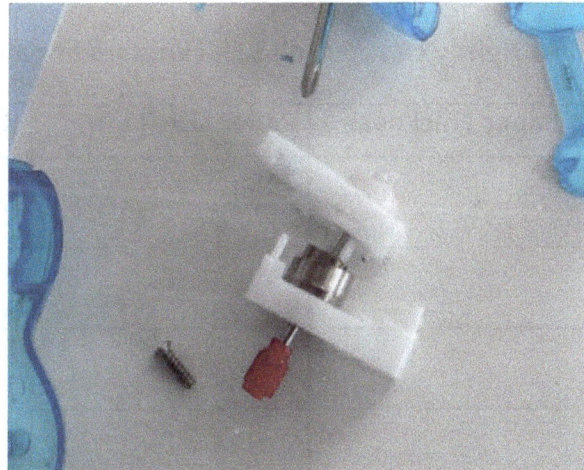

Once open, you can see that pins hold the box together in a forced fit. As the pins are pulled apart you can see a "coiled spring,"

Coiled springs get tighter and tighter as the handle is turned: this is the mechanism that causes a lot of action from a relatively few turns of the crank.

EXPLORE

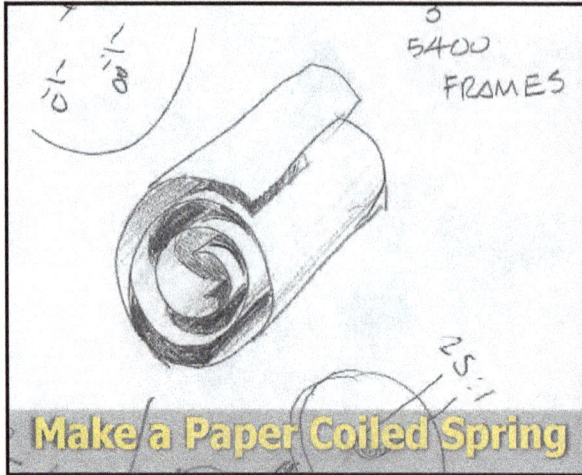

Make a Paper Coiled Spring

Mechanical advantage is a trade-off in force vs. distance. Each of the turns you make when winding up the toy provides more torque than is required to make the toy's motion (torque can be thought of as a rotational force). When winding, you input a lot of force over a little distance. The toy outputs a lot of distance that doesn't require a lot of torque.

To get a better idea of how coiled springs work, you might wind up a piece of paper – tightly – and let it go to see how the energy you put into the paper coil makes the paper spring out when released. This is the previously mysterious wind-up mechanism.

How tightly can you roll 3 thicknesses of paper?

*Paper Thickness	Paper size (l x w)	Roll Diameter	Observations
Ex: .05cm or .197cm	letter paper 215.9cm x 279.4cm 8.5in x 11in	1cm or .394inch	Measures same when rolled from short or long side

*   To measure a single sheet of paper
    1.   Stack 20 sheets of paper.
    2.   Measure the thickness of the stack.
    3.   Divide thickness by # sheets of paper to find the thickness of 1 sheet.
        Ex: 20 sheets measures 1cm
        1cm / 20 = .05cm per sheet of paper

How does this concept transfer to your toy?

EXPLORE: REVERSE ENGINEER A TOY

Prepare and Predict

- Give your project a Title.
- Explain the Purpose of this project.
- Observe the toy's motion. Talk about how you think it might operate. Once your ideas are formed, write down your prediction.
- Include observations that helped you make the prediction for your toy.

Step 1: Imagine. Predict.

Sample Prediction: How does the object store the energy you input as you turn the winder? I assume that because you wind it a little and it moves a lot, the toy must have some kind of coiled spring inside.

Take Apart
Take Notes
Collect Parts on a Paper

Now take the toy apart carefully.

- Take notes as you go.

- Also use your camera to take pictures. Though you cannot use them for your documentation, the images can be a good reminder of how it works.

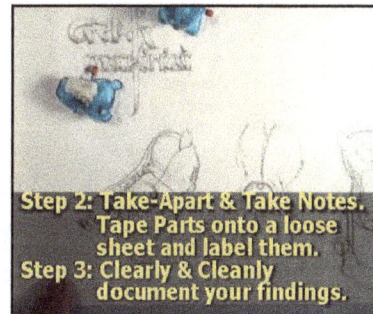

Step 2: Take-Apart & Take Notes. Tape Parts onto a loose sheet and label them.
Step 3: Clearly & Cleanly document your findings.

- Be very careful to open the toy so parts inside don't scatter or move inside the toy.

- Tape and label each part as you remove it. It is very easy to THINK you'll remember but it is also VERY easy to get confused. Tape and label AS YOU GO.

- When you think you understand how it works, and how the energy flows, document the process and clean up your sketches and flow-charts.

EXTEND

Present your findings to the group.

What can other groups add to the explanation?

Are there any constructive differences of opinion?

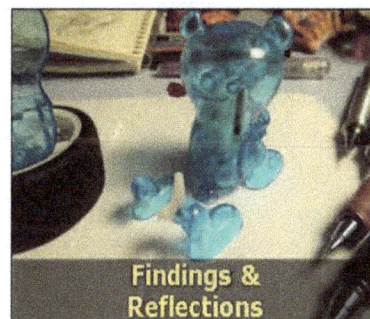

Findings & Reflections

100

Additional lessons can be found at the International STEM League website. www.insl.org

Additional lessons can be purchased from iNSL developer, Jeannie Ruiz, at her online store: Artofstemshop.com and Teacher Pay Teachers Art of STEM by Jeannie shop.

Please visit the book's website on Printing Futures website: www.printingfutures.com and send me an email with your thoughts and ideas for a more fleshed out version of the book due to publish later in the year.

Thank you for spending some of your valuable time with me as you read this book. I hope you will leave a review on my author's page on Amazon and on Goodreads. Reviews are important and I look forward to widening my network of amazing, dedicated, passionate and confident educators.

www.ingramcontent.com/pod-product-compliance
Lightning Source LLC
Chambersburg PA
CBHW080147310326
41914CB00091B/1136